GW00372648

IN ISTANBUL, WE WON IT FIVE TIMES

Welcome to the Kop Annual 2006. To celebrate our famous fifth European Cup we've hidden 20 famous faces doing the high five in the Istanbul Kop. Answers: page 2!

High five . . .

. . . and it'll come as no surprise to you that a large part of The Kop Annual 2006 is devoted to that amazing night in Istanbul. For those of you who bought the Kop Annual 2005 or regularly read the Kop Magazine, you'll know exactly what you're going to find over the next 64 pages. But to some of you we might be less familiar than the Newcastle United trophy room is with silverware – so here's what to expect. While The Kop Magazine mixes serious comment with humour, The Kop Annual 2006 should be taken about as seriously as Everton's Champions League campaign. This year, events in Turkey dominate our thoughts. You'll find Anne-field Frank's alternative road to Istanbul, Bob Benitez's adventures, a EUFA newsletter from 2012 and 'Fergie's 11' – a Manc remake of Ocean's 11 – all with a Champions League theme. We also take a look back at Kop favourite Tony Nunez's year out in Liverpool, the Lord of Frodsham Manor's rule book, give you the RAF guide to El Boss's hand signals and investigate whether some famous Liverpool cliches are in fact myths. There's also some familiar Kop features such as LFCbay, The Kop Mole's paparazzi snaps, Kop Karaoke, your Kop Summer Challenge FIVE pics, an EFC TV guide and the best of Peter King's amusing Kop cartoons. In fact you'll enjoy it so much that you might just read it Cinco Veces. For those of you not reading in Spanish, that means FIVE TIMES!

INSIDE YOUR KOP ANNUAL:

P4 Earn your wings by studying the RAF guide as seen on the Anfield runway

P6 Relive the highs and lows of our colourful journey to Istanbul

P10 Need an AC Milan Champions League winners T-shirt? Log on to Lfcbay!

P12 The banners they made for Eeeeegor

P14 See Captain Crutches salute those Anfield heroes in the Kop Summer Challenge Five

P16 A few photos from Spanish teenager Tony Nunez's exchange trip to Liverpool

P20 EUFA newsletter – exclusive

P22 Beware of the Premiership ex!

P23 The Stevie Grapevine

P24 Lord Djibril's rules of the Manor

P26 The best of Spotted

P29 Rafa's Euro telegrams

P30 Step up to the mic for Kop Karaoke

P34 No-one's safe from the Kop Mole camera

P38 The Spanish genius with a flat cap – can Rafa emulate Sir Bob?

P40 Follow Fergie's gang as they attempt to steal back the European Cup!

P45 Lonely Red hearts

P46 Watching Chelski watch us . . .

P49 A father and son tale

P50 Truth or Myth? Does Luis Garcia really drink sangria? Is there only one Michael Owen?

P54 A Toffee TV guide

P56 Ever seen Rafa with a curly mop top? See the stars before they were famous

P58 Kop letters and tips

P61 Crime report. Them Scousers again!

P62 Special version of El Anfield Arms – every Kopite's favourite boozer

P64 The Norwegian homecoming

High five answers (from opening pages): Bob Paisley, Bryan Robson and Sam Allardyce, Momo Sissoko, Jose Mourinho, David O'Leary, Bill Shankly, Rafa Benitez, Steven Gerrard, Alex Ferguson, Bono (U2), Michael Owen, Gerard Houllier, God and Shaggy (Robbie & Macca), George Bush and Tony Blair, Arsene Wenger, Hernan Crespo, Silvio Berlusconi

© Published in Great Britain in 2005 by Trinity Mirror Sport Media, PO Box 48, Old Hall Street, Liverpool, L69 3EB.

Photographic credits: Liverpool Daily Post & Echo Illustrations: Peter King Production Editor: Paul Dove
Design: Lee Ashun Writing: Chris McLoughlin Printed by Scotprint Ltd.

KOP CARTOON

Emlyn cheers on from up above as the Reds parade their fifth European Cup – with Rafa at the wheel and Bob Paisley the bus conductor. There's no room for Fergie though!

THE RAF GUIDE ✈

Rafa the gaffer has been pointing us in the right direction ever since he touched down on the Anfield runway from Valencia. His animated hand signals from the technical area steered us to the Ataturk stadium where he plotted a famous European victory. So what do the secret dug-out gestures by El Boss really mean? Earn your wings by studying this guide.

Signal: Arms stretched out wide
Most likely to be seen: During the summer (and occasionally January)
What it means: Stevie G's deciding on his future again

Signal: Little and large
Most likely to be seen: Anfield
What it means: Rafa wants Peter Crouch and Florent Sinama-Pongolle to play up front together

Signal: Taxi!
Most likely to be seen: When the transfer window has opened
What it means: Sam Allardyce has agreed to buy Diouf. One way to Bolton please!

Signal: Have you looked over there, Montse?
Most likely to be seen: In Rafa's house
What it means: I always wear my red tie with diagonal stripes on for matches and I don't like this grey one

Signal: Come 'ere
Most likely to be seen: When Milan Baros started up front in 2004/05
What it means: Milan hasn't scored again so it's time for Djibril/Nando/Flo /Gerd to have a go

Signal: What are you doing?
Most likely to be seen: When Luis Garcia has the ball
What it means: He's played a casual pass and managed to pick out the only person near him not wearing red. Again

Signal: Holding an invisible dog lead
Most likely to be seen: At Chelski
What it means: Shaun Wright-Phillips is leaving the pitch and Rafa's about to shake his hand

Signal: 'And for my next trick . . .'
Most likely to be seen: in Istanbul
What it means: I'm going to turn a 0-3 half-time deficit into a European Cup victory

Signal: Paper, scissors, stone
Most likely to be seen: In David Moores' office
What it means: If I win we buy a centre half, if you win we'll buy Michael Owen

Signal: Look at the size of that
Most likely to be seen: When Liverpool play Birmingham City
What it means: Steve Bruce has got his head stuck in the dug-out again

Signal: Too high
Most likely to be seen: In Madrid
What it means: Real Madrid are asking £16m for Michael Owen and the Geordies are daft enough to pay it

Signal: Oh My God
Most likely to be seen: At Burnley
What it means: Djimi Traore's in front of his own goal and is just about to try a Cruyff turn . . .

THE RAF GUIDE ✈

Anne-Field Frank's ALTERNATIVE road to ISTANBUL

The road to Istanbul wasn't easy in 2005 – and we're not just talking about the 10-mile hike to the Ataturk stadium. We retraced the steps of Kop diarist and veteran traveller Anne-Field Frank from Anfield to the far foreign land where we lifted European Cup number 5 . . .

START

② Atlantic Ocean: Thought we'd go and see how Rangers were getting on in their European qualifying games against CSKA Moscow but were directed here. Apparently there was less chance of them being out of their depth in the Atlantic.

⑤ Spain: Arrived in the port of La Coruna (can't understand why they're known as Deportivo) the day before the game and went out for a night on the town. They were playing that La Bamba song in all the bars which was quite funny because we've got so many Spaniards at Liverpool now. There's Rafa Benitez, Xabi Alonso, Garcia and Nunez. We could really do with a song for them all. Anyone got any ideas? Whatcha mean Josemi's been forgotten?

Monaco: Parked our pedallo next to Roman's yacht and hit the casinos the night before the match. Followed the strategy of 'always bet on 23' because Carra's having such a good season but as we were playing Pontoon it didn't really work. Left with less than £50, just enough for a pint. After the match we decided to go to Monaco Hospital. There was nothing wrong with us like, we just wanted to visit Luis, Djimi and Josemi.

④ Gibraltar: Took the opportunity to visit the British colony. They've got a big rock there and it's very impressive but doesn't look half as solid as Carra.

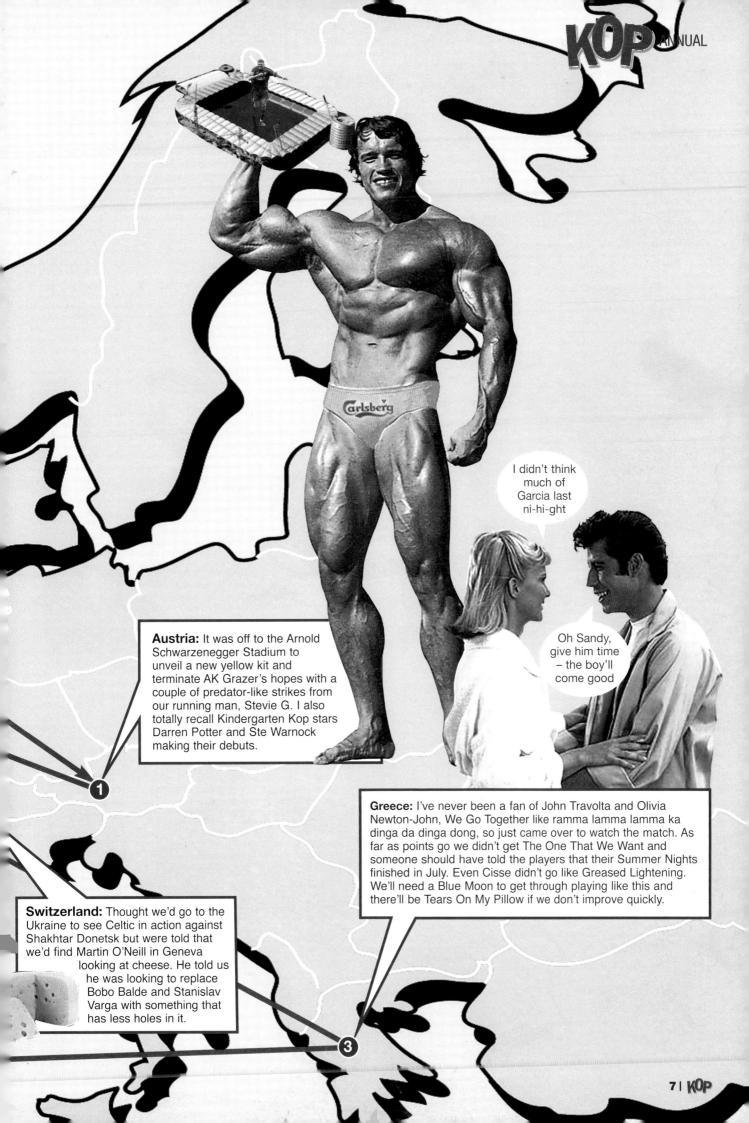

I didn't think much of Garcia last ni-hi-ght

Oh Sandy, give him time – the boy'll come good

Austria: It was off to the Arnold Schwarzenegger Stadium to unveil a new yellow kit and terminate AK Grazer's hopes with a couple of predator-like strikes from our running man, Stevie G. I also totally recall Kindergarten Kop stars Darren Potter and Ste Warnock making their debuts.

Greece: I've never been a fan of John Travolta and Olivia Newton-John, We Go Together like ramma lamma lamma ka dinga da dinga dong, so just came over to watch the match. As far as points go we didn't get The One That We Want and someone should have told the players that their Summer Nights finished in July. Even Cisse didn't go like Greased Lightening. We'll need a Blue Moon to get through playing like this and there'll be Tears On My Pillow if we don't improve quickly.

Switzerland: Thought we'd go to the Ukraine to see Celtic in action against Shakhtar Donetsk but were told that we'd find Martin O'Neill in Geneva looking at cheese. He told us he was looking to replace Bobo Balde and Stanislav Varga with something that has less holes in it.

Anne-Field Frank's ALTERNATIVE road to ISTANBUL

The Moon: Followed the precise directions of where we'll discover the Ataturk Stadium and ended up here. Might have to get in touch with NASA to get home and to warn them that we saw a space shuttle on its way to Mars. Inside were Wayne Rooney, James Beattie, David Unsworth and Mark Viduka and they all looked hungry. I fear for the Galaxy and Milky Way, too.

London: Arrived in London and while me mate went for a burger I went for a quick tour of Chelski's trophy room. Got back to him just as they were putting the ketchup on. We then spent 90 minutes sat in a stadium containing thousands of people but no noise. It was quiet enough to hear an Icelandic international drop, apart from in the away end of course.

Germany: No time to go and visit Didi's family as a few pre-match beverages needed sinking the night before in a Cologne bar with Rafa. There was no sign of Luis Garcia drinking sangria but perhaps it was because he was working as a bouncer the following night – he showed Leverkusen to the door.

Norwich: On the way down to Chelski we went along to Bernard Matthew's factory in Norfolk. Bought some of their produce which we'll send to Manchester next month as after Hernan did the Munsters it's the only sight of Turkey they'll be getting in May.

Russia: We decided to visit Russia next and climb to the top of Elbrus, the highest mountain in the whole continent. It gave us a great view across the whole of Europe and we looked really hard but we just couldn't see Arsenal at all. Then we remembered it was the quarter-finals next so it all made sense . . .

Croatia: Thought we'd pop over to Zagreb to go and visit Igor's family. They all looked like Igor – shocked to see us.

D'oh!

Istanbul: Was a bit knackered after all the travelling so gave this one a miss . . .

Italy: Didn't get the friendliest of welcomes in Turin. The match itself was something of a wildlife experiment with 10 zebras spending 90 minutes seeing if they could run through a red brick wall. Could they? Juve got to be joking.

Back | Forward | Stop | Refresh | Home | AutoFill | Print | Mail

Favorites

History

Search

Scrapbook

Page Holder

Anything and everything a Kopite exclusively made-up website and you've been promising yourself.

All Items | **Auctions** | **Buy It Now**

football magazine | Sporting Goods

☐ Search title **and** description

MANC SOULS
Bids: **1** | Time remaining: **0hrs 1min**

Thousands available. Will sell to anyone, including the devil, for large amounts, whatever the consequences

Would suit American businessman who knows nothing about soccer or tradition but wishes to transfer heavy debts and try and make a few bucks from Asian market in future

---

TACTICS TRUCK
Bids: **0** | Time remaining: **433hrs 04mins**

Heavy Goods Vehicle containing televisions, loads of wires, a couple of chairs and Andy Townsend

Been out of service for several years after previously seen parked outside football grounds. Unlikely to make Finnish individuals with mullets smile. Scrap dealers welcome

---

RED WEDDING SUIT
Bids: **9** | Time remaining: **5hrs 55mins**

One previous eccentric owner. Only worn once for wedding ceremony. Will draw attention, paparazzi, upstage bride

A once in a lifetime opportunity to purchase the most bizarre looking wedding suit that's ever been worn. Guaranteed to be totally unique

---

AC MILAN T-SHIRT
Bids: **15,000** | Time remaining: **15hrs 6mins**

Genuine Italian-made AC Milan Champions League Winners 2005 T-Shirt

Printed at half-time on May 25, 2005, this special T-shirt commemorates Milan's Champions League triumph over Liverpool in Istanbul. Thousands available

---

SCISSORS
Bids: **1** | Time remaining: **21hrs 4mins**

One pair of stainless steel scissors. Previously owned by Harry Kewell's barber in London

Item in good condition but hasn't been used for well over 12 months. Comes with special feature to reduce chances of injury when being used

---

PATRICE LUZI
Bids: **0** | Time remaining: **2 years**

Lesser spotted French goalkeeper, hardly used, last seen at Stamford Bridge in January 2003

Would suit football club who wish to avoid publicity as highly unlikely to be recognised by fans in the street. Comes with own gloves and 100% clean sheet record

---

Internet zone

wants can be found on Lfcbay. Just log on to our
bid for that red wedding suit or This Is Anfield sign
Here's just a few of the items that are on sale . . .

<u>click here</u>)

 [ ] Search <u>Refine Search</u>

MOBILE PHONE   Bids: **5**   Time remaining: **18hrs 05mins**

Nokia mobile phone, definitely not on Vodafone network. Was found on football pitch in L4 area in January '05

Phone was held by police who were handed it by a Mr W. Rooney after its owner 'mis-placed' it during a Liverpool v Man Ure game. May have suffered some damage

---

EVERTON CONTRACT   Bids: **0**   Available in January only

Three-year deal to play for Everton Football Club, prepared by Mr B Kenwright and Mr D Moyes

A Mr M. Sissoko had initially indicated he wanted the item but pulled out of the deal when he received a far better offer. Replacement owner sought

---

BROKEN DUCK   Bids: **23**   Time remaining: **23hrs 23mins**

Water bird with short legs, webbed feet and a broad, blunt bill. In need of repair

After six years and six months sitting idle, duck was broken by its owner - a Mr J. Carragher - during a trip to Lithuania

---

WHISTLE   Bids: **1**   Time remaining: **9 days**

Referee's whistle, will produce short, sharp sound at the sight of tall Scottish footballers

The referee, a Mr P. Collina, has retired and was not taken up on his offer to donate the item to the Everton F.C Museum. Would suit Mersey derby referee

---

KOP MAGAZINE   Bids: **2,398** Time remaining: **1 day 17 hours**

Best football magazine in the business written for die-hard supporters of Liverpool FC

Why pay £1.50 for The Kop magazine from the shop or by calling 0845 143 0001 when you can buy it on lfcbay at a higher price once the p&p has been added on?

THIS IS ANFIELD SIGN   Bids: **12**   Time remaining: **6 days 7 hrs**

Large, red 'This Is Anfield' sign. Formerly on wall in stadium tunnel. Great historic value for fans of L.F.C.

Because of the new arrival of 6ft 7ins striker, the sign has had to be taken down from its usual place to avoid nasty head injury. Big bargain

BISCANBUL and SUPERCROATIGORBISCANUSEDTOBEATROCIOUS
were just two Istanbul banner tributes paid to our one and only
Croatian superstar IGOR BISCAN this year. As a special thank you to
the straight-faced eastern European midfielder who sadly departed
Anfield after four and a half colourful years this summer, we've
taken some other classic Liverpool banners and given
them our own special twist . . .

Never mind the Grafton on a Friday night . . . what about this?

A ruff translation: 'Eeeeegor is the dog's b*@*!*!*'

Igor's up there with the greats after his European exploits in 2005

Our fifth European Cup in Istanbul will have gone down well back home

Igor might have confused us – but it was just his ability trying to get out

Supporters gather for their annual Eeeegor Fan Club Convention

Igor grew to be a cult figure just like Joey Jones – and he even won a European Cup too!

Not even this banner could make our deadpan Croat break into a smile

RAFA'S A GENIE-OUS

We're on our way to Istanbul and Carra's dreaming of the European Cup. Rafa's the genie in the lamp as Arsene wishes us good luck and Stevie chooses a fez

EVERY year we issue YOU with a summer challenge to get yourself in our magazine by being pictured with the The Kop at the most bizarre and far-flung locations possible. You always deliver the goods and none more so than this year when you celebrated our Champions League triumph in style. Readers were pictured holding our mag and doing a five-fingered salute from K2 to Disneyland. What's more, you even persuaded a few famous faces to join in the fun. Here's some of your pictures from the summer of '05 . . .

The Kop Magazine, Liverpool

IT'S hard to know what was more difficult. Managing to get big Sam Allardyce on the one photograph or getting the former captain of Man Ure to celebrate Liverpool's five European Cups.

Liverpool supporter Neil Clark managed both. The Maghull-based Red wasn't on his way to Istanbul though - he was feeling rather gutted as he waited to catch a flight to Florida when he bumped into the pair in Manc Airport. Over to Neil.

"In April 2004 I booked a two-week family holiday to Florida to commence on May 22, 2005. What an idiot! So on May 22, having reluctantly passed on four Champions League final tickets to my NEW friends I found myself stood in Manc Airport.

"There I spied Sam Allardyce and Bryan 'Captain Marvel' Robson and, not wishing to pass up the opportunity, I approached with Kop Magazine in hand.

"Afterwards, I had a few words with Big Sam and advised him to push through the Diouf deal pronto but to cool his interest in Didi!"

JUST hours after our Champions League success in Istanbul a Liverpool legend was getting a bit of practice in for next season by taking part in the Kop Summer Challenge Five.

Robbie Fowler has already got his message to the Man USA fans planned in advance.

Of course, when God's around, his best mate Steve McManaman is never far away and the man who won two Champions Leagues with Real Madrid was happy to join in the fun.

Kopite David Riley from Prescot is the man who persuaded the Macca and Growler partnership to become the first ex-Reds to join in the Kop Summer Challenge Five. "The picture was taken at about 5am on the morning of May 26 in the Radisson Hotel which was within spitting distance of the Ataturk Airport," said David. "It shows myself with Scooby Doo's sidekick Steve McManaman and none other than God himself, who assured me that next season when he plays at Man USA they will get the same hand signal!"

WE never thought that we'd get a couple of Man Ure players taking part in the Kop Summer Challenge, so imagine our surprise when we received these photos from Tony Flynn. The Dublin Red was in Las Vegas when he bumped into Wayne Rooney and Rio Ferdinand and persuaded both of them to hold up four fingers alongside The Kop to celebrate our four European Cup wins.

Of course, things have moved on since - we've won five European Cups. Tony claims that he's actually stood with a Klingon and a Ferengi at a Star Trek convention at the Vegas Hilton (didn't realise Johnny was related to Paris and owned a hotel) but we know Rio and Wayne when we see them - although the only surprise was that they weren't in a nightclub.

DO I not like the Kop Summer Challenge 5.

Actually, former England boss Graham Taylor thinks it's great and was more than happy to pose with Liverpool fan Ben Leather when the pair bumped into each other in Vienna Airport before the Champions League final. Wavertree-based Ben tells us that he even ended up sitting next to the man who sold us Johnny Barnes on the flight and insisted on buying him a butty and a bevvie.

"He turned out to be dead friendly and described Liverpool fans as 'the most knowledgeable in the world,' said Ben. "Yes boss. They are boss. Well said boss," said Phil Neal.

DOES this picture look familiar?

It does to us as we swear we had to climb down that mountain when we were in Istanbul to get to the Ataturk Stadium.

Travelling Kopite Mike Woolrich assures us that he was actually in Pakistan when the photo was taken and the big hill behind him is 'K2'. We were going to ask Mike why he didn't go over the hill but then we remembered Mauricio Pellegrino's performances from last season and realised that he'd already done that.

HE'S not had the nicest of receptions from the Mancs so one Liverpool fan thought it was about time that Malcolm Glazer realised that not every English football follower hates him.

Florida-based Red Bill Bullion took The Kop to 1500 Ocean Boulevard - Glazer's mansion in Palm Beach, Florida.

Dear old Malcolm didn't appear to be around so Bill simply held his palm up to remind the Salford Red Sox owner that he's paid over the odds for a club who aren't as successful as their rivals down the M62, sorry freeway.

MY YEAR OUT
(in LIVERPOOL)
By: TONY NUNEZ

AGE: 14 ¾

FROM: SPAIN

DURING 2004 aND 2005, iT WAS ArraNGED FoR me to SpEnd a yEAR iN EnglaND ONaN exCHaNge visiT WHIle aN EngLish pupIL called MicHaeL Went to MaDRid. Here arE SOME of MY pHotos...

ThIs is THE heAdmASTeR mR BENiTeZ. HE also comeS.. from SPAin and he likes possibilities →

THIS is ME stood in THE Kop and
they say they are the most ✗
knowledgable FANS in the buisness.
I think they are wrong cos they
call me Tony and I DON'T know why

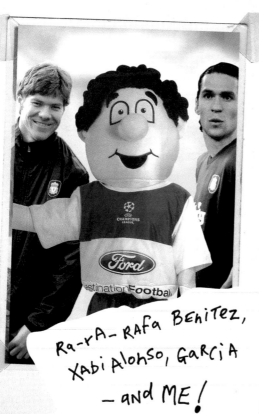

Ra-rA- RAFa BEniTEZ,
XAbi Alonso, GARCiA
- and ME!

L.f.c

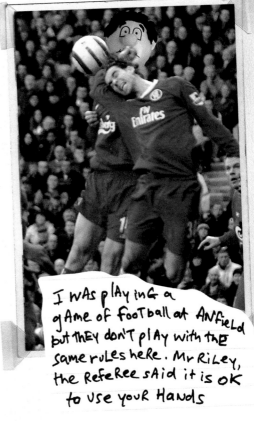

I wAs plAying a
gAme of FooTball at ANfield
but THEy don't plAy with the
same rules heRe. Mr RiLey,
the RefeRee sAid it is OK
to use yoUr Hands

THiS is ME with SoME
FRIENDS At StAmford
BRidge. It iS NICE and
PEACEful here. MY iDENtICAl
twIn aLSo CAME to visiT me

I WENt on a Day TRiP To BURNLEY
buT i diDN't likE it. I was kICkED by
anoTher boY — I THiNk hE was cALLED
RodNEY TRoTTER — so I gavE him A
shovE buT I was SENt homE EArly.

HERE is a SouvEnIR of
mY TimE in LiVERPoo1 —
a NicE shIny mEdAL
wITh 'WINNER'
ON iT !

ON a day TRiP to CARDiff
in WALES I goT to plAy foolbALL
and I ScoREd. I Got a mEdaL
foR it — buT so did ALL the oTher
boYs who Didn't scoRe

ThIs was ONE of MY
FAvouRite PLACEs in
AnfIELd. THEy gAvE mE A
sEat right nExt to The
pitch — I ofTEn sat hERE !

I.N

Here I am with other Boys In the school team. I found 'Carra' hard to understand as He doesn't speak Spanish or English.

Here Is the end of term party were the players were given a big shiny cup to keep at home!

I made some good friends at L·F·C Here I am with Lewis & Michael on holiday In Turkey

When we got Back from holiday i took my first ever busride in Liverpool. The conjestion is Terrible But the people seem very happy When the bus arrives!

EUFA

Newsletter

May 2012

MAKE THE WINNERS PAY

CHAMPIONS LEAGUE WINNERS TO FACE 12-ROUND QUALIFIER STARTING AGAINST ARMENIAN LADIES OR AMATEUR FINNISH UNDER-15s THE MORNING AFTER THE CHAMPIONS LEAGUE FINAL

—J. LOHANSSON INTERVIEW: INSIDE

MOON LINED UP TO HOST MAJOR EUROPEAN FINAL

One small step: A EUFA representative takes a look at the Moon, where the next Champions League final could be held. Right: How fans could travel to the stadium

Lunar venue can rival
Istanbul showpiece

EUFA can today announce the shortlist for the venue of the 2013 EUFA Champions League Final.

After careful consideration and some lengthy meetings in between five course luncheons in the most expensive hotel we could find, we have narrowed our selection down to three choices. They are:

1 The Moon.

After the success of the EUFA Champions League final in the Ataturk Stadium in Istanbul (2005), we have identified the Sea of Tranquility Stadium as providing similar facilities.

There will be no food or drink facilities, a barcode entry system that doesn't work, hour long queues for an insufficient number of programmes, stewards with no idea whatsoever of how to steward, piles of rubble randomly distributed around the ground and a giant marquee full of free food and alcohol for our sponsors and corporate freeloaders.

Unfortunately we cannot guarantee traffic congestion problems as there are no roads or vehicles on the moon but we will ensure that space shuttles arrive as far away from the stadium as possible and take off for earth after the game before you've had chance to get back to them.

The game will kick off at 2.41am on May 25 as this is the time when the moon is exactly over the centre of

Europe and will provide the best lighting for TV coverage.

This is currently our preferred option.

NB: Should Liverpool reach the final Lansdale Travel will be chartering a NASA space shuttle to the moon for the final. The price, including match ticket, is one million Euros. Alternatively you can catch a Happy Al's coach.

2. Kazakhstan

In 2013 football in Kazakhstan will celebrate its centenary and EUFA believes that holding the EUFA Champions League final (in association with Ford, Amstel, Sony, Mastercard and Dorothy Perkins) in the country would be an ideal way to celebrate such a landmark.

We do realise that there are logistical problems to overcome as we don't know anything about the stadiums or facilities but the fans will still go and pay through the nose wherever we play it so that doesn't

really matter.

The fact that the country borders China and would be a complete nightmare for most of Europe to get to is unfortunate but so long as there's a five-star hotel for us to use then we don't envisage a problem.

As everyone knows we only make decisions for footballing reasons and just because Kazakhstan might be looking for entry to the European Union by 2013 and hosting the EUFA Champions League final would be a huge political boost for them has got nothing to do with it.

We believe Kazakhstan would provide a good alternative to the moon.

3. Stanley Park

The new home of Liverpool Football Club has a 70,000, sorry, 60,000, sorry, 55,000 all-seater capacity.

At least it will have if it ever gets built so we've stuck it on the shortlist just in case.

Other news

EUFA would like to re-affirm that we are completely committed to stamping racism out of football.

It may appear that on occasions we say how we will impose the heaviest penalties on clubs whose supporters are involved in racist chanting but don't actually do anything. That is not the case and our new range of fines proves this.

Every time a set of fans is reported to be involved in racist chanting we will fine the club 50 cents. We have doubled this fine as it was previously 25 cents.

If this doesn't act as a deterrent then nothing will and we will continue to blame society as a whole for the problem.

In other news EUFA has ordered new carpets for our headquarters in Nyon.

We have been forced to replace the old ones as there is no space left to sweep anything else under them.

WE would like to announce the re-election of Jennart Lohansson as our president for the next two years.

Mr Lohansson is now vastly experienced and this season he fully expects to be able to pick out the Champions League captain immediately rather than try and hand the trophy to random members of the team first.

Beware of the Ex

You know the score. You go for a day out and you end up bumping into your ex. It could happen quite a bit if you're a Kopite in 2005/06. We took a look in our address book to see who we might like to see again but more importantly – who we'd like to avoid!

Baros, Milly   Birmingham   8/10
put a lot into relationship but there was
something missing so let him go
Berger, Pat   Birmingham   7/10
started like house on fire but soon faded
Diao, Salif   Portsmouth   1/10
what was I thinking?
Diouf, El-Hadji   Bolton   1/10
high maintenance and spits. Yuk.
Friedel, Brad   Blackburn   3/10
Heard good things about him but never
lived up to it. Looks better now.
Fowler, Robbie   Manchester   10/10
pure quality but seen better days
Henchoz, Steph   Wigan   9/10
honest and reliable but not stunning
Heskey, Emile   Birmingham   6/10
ok partner at times but went missing too often
James, David   Manchester   4/10
bit of a nutter
Kirkland, Chris   West Bromwich   6/10
maybe worth a call in the future
Le Tallec, Ant   Sunderland   2/10
holiday romance. looked great in France but just not the same here
Matteo, Dom   Blackburn   5/10
tried a lot of positions but was a bit of a
headless chicken and we parted amicably
Murphy, Danny   London   8/10
had a great time but relationship ran its course and had to dump him
Owen, Michael   Newcastle   10/10
top class. Want him back
Thompson, David   Blackburn   6/10
a little cracker but moved on before relationship had had time to flourish
Warner, Tony   London   0/10   ?
never got to first date
Westerveld, Sander   Portsmouth   5/10
moans a lot and always blames others
Wright, Stephen   Sunderland   6/10
going well until sent away from home by strict French guardian
Vignal, Gregory   Portsmouth   3/10
looked good when young but never matured

Come back Milly
luv Baz the Kopite

Ah . . . happy days

B
C
D
E
F
G
H
I
J
K
L
M
Mc
N
O
P
Q
R
S
T

The Stevie Grapevine

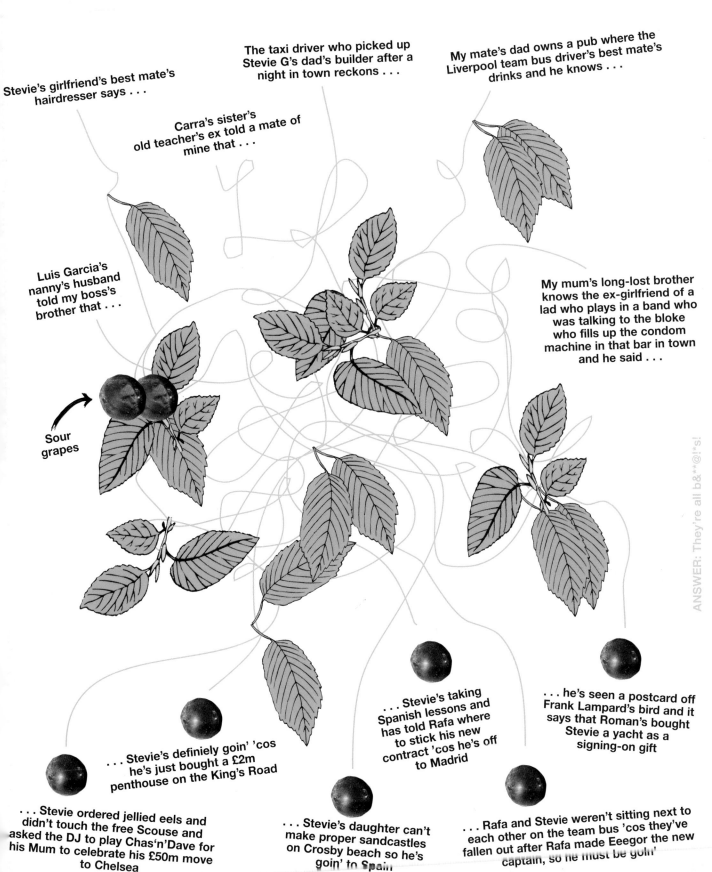

IT was a case of 'will he, won't he?' Again. And everyone thought they knew someone who knew what was gonna happen. Again. See if you can untangle the Stevie Grapevine of summer 2005 . . .

Stevie's girlfriend's best mate's hairdresser says . . .

The taxi driver who picked up Stevie G's dad's builder after a night in town reckons . . .

My mate's dad owns a pub where the Liverpool team bus driver's best mate's drinks and he knows . . .

Carra's sister's old teacher's ex told a mate of mine that . . .

Luis Garcia's nanny's husband told my boss's brother that . . .

My mum's long-lost brother knows the ex-girlfriend of a lad who plays in a band who was talking to the bloke who fills up the condom machine in that bar in town and he said . . .

Sour grapes

. . . Stevie's taking Spanish lessons and has told Rafa where to stick his new contract 'cos he's off to Madrid

. . . he's seen a postcard off Frank Lampard's bird and it says that Roman's bought Stevie a yacht as a signing-on gift

. . . Stevie's definiely goin' 'cos he's just bought a £2m penthouse on the King's Road

. . . Stevie ordered jellied eels and didn't touch the free Scouse and asked the DJ to play Chas'n'Dave for his Mum to celebrate his £50m move to Chelsea

. . . Stevie's daughter can't make proper sandcastles on Crosby beach so he's goin' to Spain

. . . Rafa and Stevie weren't sitting next to each other on the team bus 'cos they've fallen out after Rafa made Eeegor the new captain, so he must be goin'

ANSWER: They're all b&**@!*s!

WHEN Djibril Cisse bought Ridge Manor in Frodsham for £2 million in early 2005 he also inherited a title. The Liverpool striker is now officially the Lord of the Manor of Frodsham, a title which dates back to the Doomsday Book in 1086. Over the last 900 years or so the title has passed between families and was even held by Edward the Black Prince, a member of the Royal Family, in the mid-14th century. Now that Djibril the Blue Panther (his nickname back in France) owns the Manor - which has six bedrooms, four bathrooms, three stables, a ballroom, a tennis court, an indoor pool, a garage with space for six cars and a chauffeur's cottage - he's had to set a few house rules. Here art just a few of them . . .

Rules of the Manor

1) Thou shalt not use one's acreage for the purpose of hunting a reddish-brown bushy-tailed animal of the dog family known to the common peasant as a 'fox'. Hence the donning of silly red jackets is also forbode - thou wishes not for a clash with one's wedding suit - although the playing of bugles and utterances of 'tally-ho Djibril mon garcon' will be endured.

2) One's leafy driveway must be kept clear to allow one's stagecoach - a Hummer H2 with hand-crafted Louis Vuitton interior - to travel unhindered at 70 furlongs to the gallop. Knaves must ensure both sides are kept clear due to the portly size of one's corpulent vehicle.

3) Knaves and servants are required to provided a silver-star service for their Lord and his wench at all feast times. Should one's spit-roasted pig perchance be less than succulent and one's salt not be passed to precisely the exact point by one's servant thou shall, alas, be forced to waft one's arms in the air, berate one's knave and slowly walk away from one's dining table muttering untold expletives in a fit of pique.

4) When one's hairdresser or one's tattooist is in residence with one's Lordship, knaves are dutifully requested not to laugh like ninnys at thee's latest haircut or cross each other's palms with silver and run a book on which body part one's latest tattoo will cover. Hence, such insubordination would result in knaves visiting the Frodsham job centre over yonder.

5) By nature of thou's large acreage, one appreciates that others may request to uses one's plot for the purpose of sporting events. Alas, thou shall not be permitted to use Ridge Manor for cheese rolling, the Eton Wall Game, rugger, chariot racing or parlour games in the grand ballroom. However, thee will allow the kicking of a pig's bladder around in a grassy area on the proviso that his Lordship is considered the star participant. Should thee not get the service one demands...see rule three.

6) At special supper times, whenever one is presented with a silver cup, servants must hold it while one performs an unnecessary and embarrassing dance in front of it whilst other guests look on in a bemused manner.

Sami **Hyypia** at Tina Marriott's horse yard in Maghull.

Ex-Reds **Michael Thomas** and **Mark Walters** arriving at Anfield together to watch the Arsenal game.

Liverpool fan and former Farm frontman **Peter Hooton** looking at wardrobes in IKEA.

Former Arsenal midfielder **Charlie George** having a meal at trendy Bar 52 on Lark Lane after seeing the Gunners beaten at Anfield.

Abel Xavier strolling down Old Hall Street, Liverpool.

Xabi Alonso buying a sandwich in a café at one of the departure lounges at John Lennon International airport.

Ex-Everton players **Mick Lyons** and **John Bailey** drinking in Rigby's, Dale Street, on The Kop's Christmas night out.

Former Tranmere defender **Richard Jobson** buying duty free at the airport in Cuba.

Vladimir Smicer in Cranberry's coffee shop, Southport.

Steve McMahon in Competitive Edge menswear shop, Southport, looking at jeans.

Igor Biscan in the Allerton Tesco, buying a pineappple.

Former Cast frontman **John Power**, dressed in army gear and sporting a huge beard, walking up the Main Stand steps at the Chelski semi-final.

Chelski striker **Arjen Robben** and a bloke in an Erik Meijer shirt going wild as **Raymond van Barneveld** swept all before him at the BDO World Darts championships at The Lakeside, Essex.

Rafael Benitez and **Fernando Morientes** chatting while having a meal in Est Est Est.

John Arne Riise signing a mirror in city centre hairdressers Scissor Kicks after having his hair cut there.

Phil Thompson having a meal in the Hope Street Hotel's Carriage Works Restaurant.

We have the Power: John Arne Riise's mate

John Arne Riise watching his mate Phil 'The Power' Taylor take part in a darts tournament in Stoke.

Jamie Carragher saying farewell to Villa-bound **Milan Baros** with a hug in Mosquito.

Zak Whitbread, Richie Partridge, Jon Otsemobor, David Mannix, Djimi Traore's Danish girlfriend and **Bruno Cheyrou's** wife at the Radisson Hotel's 1st birthday party on Old Hall Street.

Mark Wright enjoying a meal at the Sandpiper, Bickerstaffe, near Ormskirk.

Salif Diao and **Emile Heskey** shunning the Birmingham nightlife in favour of the Blue Bar at the Albert Dock.

Jan **Molby**, David **Fairclough**, Alan **Kennedy** and **Mark Walters** deep in conversation inside the Birmingham City press room.

Man City coach **Stuart Pearce** sat in the Main Stand taking notes during Liverpool's win over Bayer Leverkusen.

Djimi Traore dropping off some clothes at Johnson's cleaners on Dale Street.

John Arne Riise shopping in Cricket, Cavern Walks, on a day that Alex Curran and Coleen McLoughlin weren't in there.

Luis Garcia and his family enjoying a meal in La Vina, North John Street.

Jamie Carragher and his mates in Liverpool's Chinatown district celebrating his Liverpool Echo Merseyside Sports Personality of the Year award.

Zak Whitbread being refused entry to Liverpool club 'Mood' on St Patrick's night because he was wearing trainers.

Zak Whitbread in Modo, Concert Square, after the Bolton game.

Former Liverpool midfielder **Nigel Spackman** deep in conversation with **Sam Allardyce** outside the Anfield press room ahead of the Reds' win over Bolton.

Igor Biscan signing autographs on Victoria Street and smiling as

Old star haunt: Big Emile and Salif were also spotted in the Blue Bar in Liverpool's Albert Dock

The Kop Mole has got spies all over the place and nothing escapes his watchful eye. Whether it's Brian McFadden singing 'We all dream of a team of Carraghers' in Aldo's Place or John Arne Riise watching the darts, our Mole is on the scene to keep you up to date on the whereabouts of the Redmen (and others) when they're off duty.
Here's a few GENUINE sightings from this year . . .

Aldo's bar: Scene of Brian McFadden's sing-song

passers-by chanted 'Eeeeeegor' as he tried to put money into a pay-and-display parking machine.

Juventus legend **Paolo Rossi** having lunch in Bella Italia, Ranelagh Street before the Champions League game at Anfield.

Fabio Capello and minders stood admiring the John Lennon statue on Mathew Street on the same day.

Djimi Traore at Johnson's Cleaners (again) on Victoria Street.

Phil Thompson looking lost as he walked around the front entrance to the Liverpool Echo on Old Hall Street.

Everton defender **Alessandro Pistone** watching some live Champions League football at Anfield from the Main Stand.

Brian McFadden sat in the Paddock for the same game.

Middlesbrough boss **Steve McClaren** outside the Radisson Hotel on Old Hall Street before the Juve game.

Paco Herrera walking down Dale Street chatting in Spanish on his mobile phone.

Chris Kirkland playing golf at Mossock Hall Golf Club, near Ormskirk, while his team mates were playing football at Selhurst Park.

Stevie Gerrard watching **John Higgins** play **Mark Selby** at the World Snooker Championships at The Crucible, Sheffield.

Djibril Cisse with his Mum and daughter leaving Melwood in his new white Hummer H2 sport utility vehicle and, on a different day, getting a parking ticket while shopping in Cricket.

UEFA president **Lennart Johansson** in Specsavers, Lord Street before the Chelski game after leaving his glasses in Sweden (see below!).

Brookside's **Ron Dixon** (Vince Earl) laughing and joking with ex-Red David Johnson in the Main Stand car park after the Boro game.

Steven Gerrard, Jamie Carragher, Steve Finnan, John Arne Riise, Florent Sinama-Pongolle, Kenny Dalglish, Euan Blair celebrating the win over Chelski in Mosquito.

Radio One's **Colin Murray** among the travelling Kop at Fratton Park.

Xabi Alonso driving down Castle Street in his Porsche Cayenne.

Coronation Street's **Candice** (Nikki Sanderson) stood just inside Anfield's main entrance after the Chelski game.

Former Liverpool stars **Kenny Dalglish, Alan Hansen, Roy Evans, John Toshack, John Aldridge, David Fairclough, Jan Molby, Alan Kennedy, Bruce Grobbelaar, Steve McManaman, Gary Gillespie, Ian St John, Tommy Smith, Brian Hall, Steve Heighway, Michael Owen, Ian Rush and Steve Staunton** at Anfield for the Chelski Champions League game (and they're just the ones we saw!).

Steven Gerrard and his mates in The George in Crosby after Liverpool's win over Aston Villa.

Jamie Carragher riding a bike along Crosby beach and almost getting knocked off it by a puppy who inadvertently ran into his path.

Josemi leaving a chemists on Smithdown Road in Wavertree.

Igor Biscan driving down Islington in his left-hand drive Croatian G-Wagon. **Djibril Cisse** and **Djimi Traore** sat in their vehicles outside CSL on Speke Retail Park.

Jamie Carragher pushing a pram near to his home in Blundellsands.

Milan Baros chatting on his mobile phone outside the Living Room on the Friday before the Champions League final. **Milan** and **Vladi** wearing their Champions League winners' medals and signing autographs in Manchester Airport after we'd won!

Jamie Carragher out in town deservedly celebrating our Champions League success on Bank Holiday Monday in May with Liverpool boxer Paul Smith and their mates.

Carra's mate: Paul Smith (right) with Paul Dalglish and boxer Ricky Hatton in Liverpool's Newz bar

Anthony Le Tallec in The Quarter, Falkner Street.

Former Westlife member **Brian McFadden** singing 'We all dream of a team of Carraghers' in Aldo's Place, Victoria Street, hours after the homecoming parade through the city centre.

Ray Houghton booking into a hotel near Lansdowne Road, Dublin, before commentating on the Republic of Ireland's 2-2 draw with Israel.

KOP CARTOON

With Fabio Capello's Juventus despatched, it was time to get revenge against Chelski for the Carling Cup final – so Xabi and Rafa cooked up something special for Jose and Frank . . .

LFC TELEGRAMS AND NOTICEBOARD

El Boss got many letters of congratulations after our great win in Istanbul (including a strange one from Fergie). Here's a few other silly ones that were mailed to Rafa's office this summer

---

LIVERPOOL FOOTBALL CLUB Date: 27.05.05   WESTERN UNION | MAILGRAM

I'm proud of my boys.

Gerard Houllier

Congratulations Mr Benitez. I would have loved to have had the privilege to have refereed such a wonderful final before I retire. I'm sure I will enjoy one more great occasion before I hang up my whistle. P.S. I'm looking forward to refereeing the Villarreal v Everton game.

Pierluigi Collina

Man. I need some advice on comebacks. Give me a call dude.

Mike Tyson

To reply by Mailgram Message, see reverse side for Western Union's toll-free numbers.

Well done la! I can get you a blag Gucci watch for twenty notes, no questions asked.
A mate of a taxi driver who knows Montse's hairdresser

We have reason to believe your fans and players owe us millions of pounds.

**Mr R. O'Fire
(acting on behalf of the
Johnny Cash estate)**

B@$+@£*$

Paolo Maldini

WESTERN UNION TELEGRAM

What a night. Oh dear, I've missed the 'K' off just like I did with Roger and Bob.

The Queen

Well done. Can't believe I missed out. Call if you need me. I'll be waiting. If I'm not in try my mobile as I may be away on a short holiday in Newcastle.

Michael Owen

I've got to hand it you and your team. Come to think of it, I did.

Andriy
Shevchenko

Congratulations and by the way, got any tips on penalty shoot-outs for next year?
The FA, Lancaster Gate

Well done Rafa. That really was a miracle. How Harry Kewell managed to run at full speed at the final whistle after limping off in the first half was amazing. Can you do anything for me as I suffer from terribly sore feet - especially when the going gets tough.
W. Alkon, Withope, Inyerarts

Congratulations - you owe us one!
Ken and Deirdre Barlow
The Welsh Rugby Union team
The new Doctor Who
The new Pope

American Guy (With apologies to Don McLean)

A long, long time ago
I can still remember
How Man United used to
make them smile
But I knew that if they had their chance
That they would take a cash advance
And, maybe, make a
million from their pile

But Malcolm's offer made them shake
They saw how much that
they would make
Good news on the doorstep
They had to take that final step

I can't remember if I cried
When Liverpool won number five
But something touched me deep inside
The day Uni-ted died

So buy-buy, some American guy
Drove his chevy to Old Trafford
Made the Stretford End cry
And them Scousers again
were drinking Istanbul dry
Singin' 'this'll be the day United die.
This'll be the day United die'.

Did you sell your shares for love
Or was Glazer's offer just too much
Did your conscience tell you to?
Do you believe in Super Bowl
Do three quid buy your mortal soul
And can you teach me
how to kick field goals?

Well I know that you're in love with him
'Cos I saw you
all just caving in

You shrugged off your values
Man, you're worse than Roman's Blues

Now that ugly Yank from Tampa Buck
Transferred his debts, put your prices up
But you just didn't give a ****
The day Uni-ted died
And we're all singin' . . .

Bought by some American guy
Let the Yanks fill your banks
But not Murdoch and Sky
And them Scousers again
were drinking Istanbul dry
Singin 'this'll be the day United die.
This'll be the day United die'.

Annie (Road)'s Song
(With apologies to John Denver)

We followed you blindly
Up the mountains to Grazer
Through the heat
out in Athens
For a p**s up in Spain
Out in Cologne with Rafa
Dodging missiles in Turin
Oh, Liverpool FC
You've thrilled us again

We'll cherish our memories
Of those Monaco prices
Of our knees-up at Chelsea
Of the noise on the Kop
Of the glory in Turkey
Of our homecoming party
Oh Liverpool FC
We've won it again

Nah nah
nah nah
nah nah
FIVE!

Nah nah
nah nah
nah nah
FIVE!

Repeat to fade

AMERICAN GUY

ANNIE (ROAD)'S SONG

PELLEGRINO

The Kop has always had dreams and songs to sing. Whether it's celebrating the glory round the Fields of Anfield Road or just having a chortle at United (States), Anfield's famous 12th Man enjoys a tune or two.

(We've got Mauricio) Pellegrino
(With apologies to Tony Christie and Peter Kay)

Sha la la lala lalala Pelle!
Sha la la lala lalala Pelle!
Sha la la lala lalala Pelle!
Pellegrino plays for me.

We've got Mauricio Pellegrino
Although we think that he's a bit slow

Maybe he's over the hill-o
But Pellegrino plays for me

Sha la la lala lalala Pelle!
Sha la la lala lalala Pelle!
Sha la la lala lalala Pelle!
Pellegrino plays for me.

Rafalution
(With apologies to the Beatles again)

You say you want a
Rafalution, well you know,
we all went to Istanbul.
You say it's only evolution,
well you know, that's just
Houllier talking bull.
He paid £10m for El-Hadji
Diouf and Salif never
would have won
us the Cup . . .
Don't you know it's
gonna be alright

You say you want a
Rafalution, well you know,
we all wanna win the league.
The next step in our
evolution, well we know,
Stevie's doin' what he can.
But when you want
money for men like
Michael Owen, don't you
know that you can
count us out . . .
Hope it's gonna be alright

Nottingham Forest
(To the tune of 'Lady Madonna' with apologies to Lennon and McCartney)

Nottingham Forest, Europe at your feet,
Wonder how you've managed
to sink so deep.
Megson and Kinnear,
worse than David Brent
Season tickets have all
been dumped in the Trent.
David Platt arrived without a licence
He was even worse than big fat Ron
Paul Hart ran the club on
just a shoestring,
now it's League One . . .
Nottingham Forest,
twice were Europe's best,
Now you've sunk much
lower than all the rest.

(instrumental)

Now it's League One.
Nottingham Forest, shirts and faces red
Never been the same without
Old Big 'Ead.

(instrumental)

Your demise is never ever ending,
Cloughie's glory days are
now long gone,
ITV Digital stopped you spending,
now it's League One.
Nottingham Forest, Europe at your feet
Wonder how you've managed
to sink so deep.

The importance of Being Rio
(With apologies to Oasis)

I'll sell my soul for another time
'Cos the Mancs, they won't pay me
I begged my chairman for a pay rise
He said "Son, the debt's rising"

Then Malcolm called me the other night
He said "Man, you'll fleece me
The fans all told me to **** right off
They said "boy, you greedy"

But I won't sign
As long as there's a million quid
that isn't mine, I'll still whine
Oh it's not fair innit
I ain't got a limit
If I don't get my rise then
my heart's not in it

I won't sign
As long as there's a million quid
that isn't mine, I'll still whine
Oh it's not fair innit
I ain't got a limit
If I don't get my rise then
my heart's not in it

I lost my licence in the
summertime
'Cos I don't stop speeding
The bizzies clocked me at 105
Almost a rec-ord reading

I begged the drug testers
for some more time
They said "Son, you're
not playing"
The FA banned me for
eight whole months
But I still wanted paying

I won't sign
As long as there's a million
quid that isn't mine
I'll still whine
Oh it's not fair innit
I ain't got a limit
If I don't get my rise then
my heart's not in it

Here's a few examples of what happened when we stepped up to the mic after supping a beer or five on the road to Turkey. It was red faces all round the morning after – but at least we didn't do the Cisse dance. All together now . . .

NOTTINGHAM FOREST

THE IMP OF BEING RIO

RAFALUTION

KOP
A TEAM OF CARRAGHERS

Pictured top row, left to right: Jamie Carragher, Jamie Carragher, Jamie Carragher, Jamie Carragher. Middle row: Jamie Carragher, Jamie Carragher, Jamie Carragher, Jamie Carragher, Jamie Carragher, Jamie Carragher. Front row: Jamie Carragher, Jamie Carragher, Jamie Carragher, Jamie Carragher (captain), Jamie Carragher, Jamie Carragher, Jamie Carragher

Graphic: Lee Ashun

THE KOP MOLE'S PAPARAZZI PICS

It takes dedication to get the photos the papers want. Working 24 hours a day for that special snap of a famous face is no easy job. Over the past 12 months, our very own Kop Mole has left no stone unturned in his pursuit of the hottest celebrity pictures. Here's just a few . . .

The Sunday papers are always trying to stitch up Wayne Rooney for going to the chippy or for a burger but I got a picture (above) that really stunned them – the boy wonder himself heading for a health food shop! And here's another picture that shocked football fans across the country (top left). I captured El-Hadji Diouf . . . wearing normal clothes. Lastly, this snap (left) was plastered all over the papers – it shows Alex Curran and Colleen McLoughlin NOT shopping at exclusive designer shop Cricket. Strange but true – the camera never lies.

Here's a snap that you never thought you'd see. I captured Arsene Whinger and Swir Alex Ferguson at a summer fete where they enjoyed each other's company for hours on end. They even agreed to take part in a friendly tug of war with the Premiership trophy

You have it Alex

No, no - after you, Arsene, I insist

STAR, Wednesday, September 1

Jose coat shocker! That was the headline that went with this picture (left) when I caught Mourinho buying a jacket from Matalan. And here's us thinking he was a Prada man! A couple of days later, I got lucky again and captured Djibril Cisse out jogging (below left). He was injured at this time and had actually gone three weeks without a trip to the hairdresser's. Another picture that impressed the press boys was this one, below. It's a big game in the Premiership and I was there to capture the moment that Sven Goran Eriksson DIDN'T turn up. Now that's dedication!

Sven's seat

PETER CROUCH
SIGNS FOR
THE EUROPEAN
CHAMPIONS

KOP POSTER

We won it for sure but now we must think about winning the next one. There's no bigheads here

After winning his first European Cup at Liverpool, young Spanish boss Rafael Benitez was desperate to emulate the great Bob Paisley by winning it again . . .

Any sangria, like?

The trophies and manager of the month awards started to fly in - but for some reason, another rival manager was awarded a knighthood instead of him

Like most things in my life, Roman fixed it for me

Disillusioned about not being made 'Sir Bob', the Reds boss decided to retire from the game and said his goodbyes to the players - including Luis Garcia

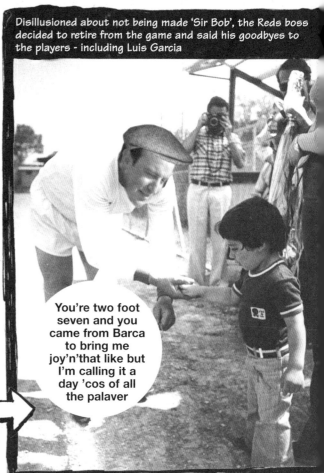

You're two foot seven and you came from Barca to bring me joy'n'that like but I'm calling it a day 'cos of all the palaver

Sound as a pound

Does this look better senor Aldo?

After taking advice off Liverpool legend Aldo, he changed his name to Bob and bought a big woolly jumper to help him think like the former Anfield manager

There are possibilities if you pass it to thingy-me-jig, like

He abandoned his usual place on the touchline and stuck to the dugout, where he wore slippers, read the Racing Post and tried to talk to his players like Paisley would

Bob Benitez even bought a Spanish hard man with a muzzy and an extrovert Zimbabwean goalkeeper - and bought himself a mac and flat cap to lead the team out

Will I get booked for doing a handstand?

Are yoo lookin' a'me senor? Gizza job per favor!

Eeeeeh. I'd sooner be pickin' a winner at Sandown

Montse could do with a new watch

Can't you leave your cups at home for just one day Bob?

Bob Benitez spent his afternoons chatting in the park with friends but his mind started to drift back to Anfield

Liverpool were struggling under their new Spanish hard man boss who had taken over the reins from Benitez and the Anfield crowd was getting restless

El Souey out! Bring back Bob!

The cappuccino cups will fly at half-time for sure senors!

El Souey was sacked and Benitez returned to Anfield - but decided to call himself Rafa again. Another European Cup followed after a Stevie G hat-trick in the final against Chelsea

What's happened to Rafa, la?

THE END

FERGIE'S ~~OCEAN'S~~ 11

Cast

Alex Ferguson (Danny Ocean) the ringleader   **Roy Keane** (Rusty Ryan) the right-hand man
Wayne Rooney (Linus Caldwell) the new kid on the block   **Rio Ferdinand** (Basher Tarr) the Cockney wide-boy
Tim Howard (Livingston Dell) the American geek   **Ruud van Kneestillsore** (Frank Catton) the con-man
Malcolm Glazer (Reuben Tishkoff) the bank-roller   **Bobby Charlton** (Saul Bloom) the old boy
Gary & Phil Neville (Turk & Virgil Malloy) the brothers   **Cristiano Ronaldo** (Yen) the grease man

Also starring

Rafa Benitez (Terry Benedict) the empire builder
European Cup (Tess Ocean) the prized possession

Alex Ferguson

Alex is the boss, the ringleader and the man with the plan to try and get back what he wants most of all - the European Cup.

Roy Keane

Roy is Alex's right-hand man, a trusted confidante who often does his boss's talking for him.

Wayne Rooney

Wayne is the talented newcomer who has a legacy to live up to and, as a Scouser, a reputation for being able to lift anything.

Rio Ferdinand

Rio is the Cockney wide-boy whose job is to make the Anfield lights become like him - a bit dim - so the heist can be carried out.

Tim Howard

Tim is the American geek and the group's surveillance expert as he's used to watching balls fly past him into the net.

Ruud van Kneestillsore

Ruud is the conman of the group and is there to see if his unique penalty winning skills can be utilised to sneak his way inside Anfield.

Malcolm Glazer

Malcolm is bankrolling the operation as he wants the cup in his Salford Red Sox museum so he can charge fans $20 a time to see it.

Bobby Charlton

Bobby is the retired old pro who provides the link to a by-gone era and can't resist getting involved rather than stay out of the limelight.

Gary & Phil Neville

The brothers Grim are odd-job men of the team although no-one can quite understand how they've got there in the first place.

Cristiano Ronaldo

Cristiano is the agile grease-man whose job is to use his acrobatics to unlock doors others can't.

Rafa Benitez

Rafa has successfully rebuilt the Liverpool Empire through hard work but his success has made Alex jealous and out to get him.

European Cup

After an eight year marriage to Liverpool, the European Cup sought a divorce in 1985 and had affairs across Europe including a brief fling with Alex in 1999 but has now realised what it was missing and has decided to settle down on Merseyside for good.

The plot.

Alex is a man with a plan. Rafa has the one thing he craves most of all - the European Cup. Alex had it in his hands back in the summer of '99 but let it slip through his grasp and then had to watch as Rafa's XI acquired the trophy on behalf of Liverpool FC in Istanbul. Now, with it on permanent display in the Anfield museum, Alex wants it back but with no hope of winning it on the pitch it leaves him with only one option. In one night, Alex's hand-picked 11 man crew of specialists will attempt to steal Rafa's glittering trophy by infiltrating the maximum security Anfield Museum and taking the cherished cup back down the East Lancs Road to Castle Greyskull. They'll have to risk all to pull off the daring heist but if they don't, the trophy they won on the greatest night in their entire history will remain at the home of their hated rivals forever ...

The plan.

1. Alex convinces Malcolm to bankroll the whole scheme.

Malcolm is reluctant at first. He's already heavily in debt and costs will be high. Rio wants £100,000 an hour, Wayne's lunch bill will run into five figures and Bobby wants to be involved in the ticket selling operation if they make a movie about it and show it in one of their Red Cinemas. But Alex makes Malcolm come round when he tells him how much he could charge for fans to see the cup in his museum and he gives Alex a strict budget to work from.

2. Alex gets his team together.

He needs a right-hand man, a grease man, a con-man, a geek and an expert thief. As he's manager of Manchester United, they aren't hard to find.

3. The recce. They need to know the lay-out of the museum and the security provisions. Alex turns to Incey, an old colleague who cleverly infiltrated Anfield a few years back and who can still get access to the museum now as it contains the shirt he was wearing when he decided to come off late on during a vital Man Ure v Liverpool cup tie at Castle Greyskull in 1999 (which swung the game in Alex's favour). Incey's information shows that the cup is kept in a bullet-proof, unbreakable case inside the museum at the Kop end of Anfield. Moving red lasers surround the case, which is also alarmed. There are three locked doors to negotiate to get into the museum and before that the steel Paisley Gates. Two security guards patrol outside.

4. Alex puts his plan into action.

a) Gary will drive Rio's American Sports Utility vehicle to Anfield with the others hiding in the back. The vehicle has been chosen as it is big and has low mileage as Rio hasn't been allowed to drive it for some time now. Phil will follow in the getaway vehicle - an open top tour bus - which will go unnoticed by locals as they're so used to seeing one travel down Walton Breck Road.
b) Once parked up, several of the team will leave the vehicle and carry out their individual tasks.
c) Rio will break into Anfield and a local electricity sub-station. At a pre-planned time, he will cut the power so the lights, lasers and alarm don't work for 30 seconds until the back-up generator kicks in. Tim will go with him and, using his natural handling skills, connect a laptop to the sub-station circuit board so he can intercept the CCTV pictures.

d) Cristiano will shimmy his way up the flagpole in flag-pole corner, dive on to the Kop roof, step-over the stray footballs left from when El-Hadji Diouf had shooting practice and, using those bizarre bits of string he used to have in his hair, climb down into the stadium.
e) Ruud and Bobby will distract the security guards. Ruud will pretend that he's actually a cousin of talking horse Mr Ed and has escaped from Aintree Racecourse, which will cause the guard to faint with shock, while Bobby will regale the other security guard with tales of how he won the World Cup in 1966 until the bloke falls asleep through boredom.

5. Getting in.

Whilst all that is going on, Alex, Roy and Wayne will make their way into the museum through the front door using a unique and sophisticated technique - Roy will kick, punch and head-butt the door, and then the other two inside, until they have been broken down.

6. Nicking the Cup.

The three men will meet Ronaldo in the trophy room and when Rio cuts the power the following will happen. Ronaldo will dive on top of the glass case and place a cd-player and speakers on top before turning up the volume and pressing play. As Posh Spice's latest single plays out the supposedly unbreakable glass will begin to crack and as it does Roy will launch into an 'Alf Inge Haaland' style tackle which will be enough to ensure it shatters.
Quick as a flash Wayne will then grab the silver cup and shove it up his jumper - as no-one will notice the extra bulge - before they all make for the exit door. While this is going on, Alex will monitor his stop-watch to ensure it all happens in the 30 seconds available.

7. Getting away.

The entire crew will meet back on the bus and, using his versatility, Phil will drive it back down the East Lancs to Salford where Alex will spend the night with it before it is put proudly on display in Malcolm's museum.

The Outcome. How it all went wrong . . .

1) Things got off to a bad start when Fergie's XI got into Rio's car and the paparazzi immediately followed. As a result they had to ditch it for a more inconspicuous vehicle. They ended up piling into Alex's Jag and went down the M62 which meant they could use the hard shoulder all the way to Liverpool.

2) Rio got into the electricity sub-station but Tim didn't. The American got half-way there, but decided to go back to Alex's Jag again only to find himself in no-man's land. He was last seen in Stanley Park sitting on a bench, a feeling he knows only too well.

3) Cristiano made his way on to the Anfield roof but after stepping over a stray football felt a pigeon brush past his leg and flung himself 100 feet to the ground, remonstrating at the corner flag to show the offending bird a yellow card.

4) Ruud and Bobby both had trouble with the security. The first security guard had put £50 on Ruud to win at Haydock a couple of weeks earlier and performed a citizen's arrest, refusing to let the long-faced Dutchman leave until he paid him back. Bobby was just getting the other security guard to drop off when a freak gust of wind blew his comb-over clean off and he was forced to chase it up the alley-way next to The Albert.

5) Roy's head was enough to break the doors down and get into the museum but once inside, the problems started when Rio forgot that they were all inside Anfield and cut the power for Goodison Park.

1999 final through suspension he didn't know how to pick it up and left empty handed.

10) He and Alex legged it to the open top bus but found it on bricks with the windows smashed and Phil in tears. Phil had not paid his £2 to a 10-year-old kid who'd asked to 'mind yer open top bus mate' and he ran off to join another outfit destined for failure just a few yards away from Anfield.

And so Fergie's XI failed to pull off their heist. Like most of their European campaigns, they left empty handed and the European Cup remained with Rafa at its Anfield home, where it shall remain FOREVER.

6) As a result all the alarms went off and with Ronaldo still refusing to get up from the pitch unless someone brought a stretcher on, there was no cd player to play Posh Spice's latest hits.

7) That meant Alex had to resort to giving the glass case the hairdryer treatment and amazingly it melted the glass.

8) All that was needed now was for Wayne to grab the silver trophy but he was nowhere to be seen. Unfortunately, he'd heard a rumour that McDonald's had left a box full of chicken nuggets when they'd vacated their old premises next door and had gone in there to find them.

9) Roy tried to grab the trophy instead but after missing the

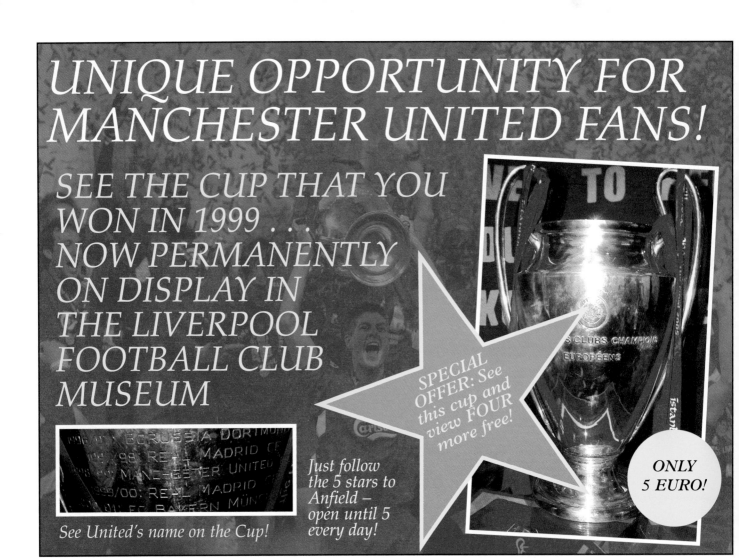

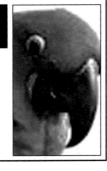

Perfect Match

Featuring NEW ADS!

JOHN ARNE RIISE has found himself taking a bit of stick after his rather unusual approach to chatting up women.

Our former topless Norwegian, who recently split from wife Guri, sent a generic text message to 15 different models and glamour girls asking for a date.

It said: "I have always thought you charming, cute, sexy. I will ask you out for a romantic dinner. Kiss from John Arne Riise."

That didn't go down very well with all the women – but his Mum spoke out in his defence.

"Yes, my son is on the lookout but he's single now and I can't understand any girl being upset," she said.

We say good luck to John but after all the trouble Goldenbrains had with texting perhaps he should stick to a more traditional approach – the good old lonely hearts adverts.

Of course, as all of us can get a bird (er, that's woman - PC Ed) we wouldn't have a clue how to write a lonely hearts ad.

So we scoured the paper and found these adverts to give JAR a few ideas on how to woo the ladies.

CANNOCK Male, 34 , author, OHAPC, likes me, me and me, WLTS famous female or couples in PCP for DW after midnight. Ego massager preferred.

ENGLAND, YK, football, YK, captain, YK, 30, YK, Madrid based, YK, low IQ, YK, dull voice, YK, likes PS, YK, being famous, YK, texting GAP, YK, SSS, YK, saying you know, YK, dislikes PS singing, YK, people stealing limelight, YK, Fergie, YK, seeks, YK, SSS, YK, for texting, YK, and newspaper coverage, YK.

RUSSIAN billionaire, N/S, OMAYAFC, seeks footballers for WD. Likes Chelski FC, money-making, paying over the odds.

FAT Scouser, 19, OABAAM, Manchester based, likes S&M, pies, chips, gravy, eating in and out, seeks granny, 50-75, for discreet fun. Will pay.

PETER, 50, balding, arrogant, successful businessman, WLTM male footballers 18-30 in up-market restaurants leading to LTDWM. Will travel to Liverpool, Manchester, North London, Lyon.

FIERY Scot, 52, well travelled now in NUT, well dressed, LLMAY, likes C&A, WLTB a TCS to replace TOS. Currently in rocky relationship, CGSS.

Match found

SOUR-faced Scot, early 60s, old-fashioned, OKMTB, likes M&S, chewing gum, fitbae, getting things my own way, seeks males, any nationality, 17-30, for HDT.

ARE you DT? Did you arrange to meet male, 26, from Manchester? Sorry. I forgot TTU and AMP. Please call again.

ARROGANT London-based Portuguese male, 41, grey hair, AMEX holder, high self-opinion, CFM, still seeks LC for F&F with FF.

SILVER fox, 60s, been OTS, since disastrous STR with EFC and SAG in 1990s, seeks Male/female CP to GAJ. All offers considered.

EX-Con, 33, OTAK, 6ft tall, piercing eyes, Scottish roots now Merseyside based, likes pigeons, nights in FAW and nights out FAM, aggro, red cards and BP dislikes burglars, seeks GC for OYCE on IWP.

MATCH OF THE DAY

JAR, Norwegian male, 24, separated, OCLWM, Liverpool based, GSOH, likes playing football, GITB scoring, going topless, CLAW, plenty of stamina, WLTT cute, sexy, FAF, models and glamour girls, 20-26, for RD and TWIT. Will reply to all texts.

BORING balding Geordie, 35, footballer and OP for SKY, NITWIT, likes being dull, CBF, nights in, dislikes excitement, nights out, Roy Keane, WLTM CB in a DA to RTTM. No text messages please.

ARE you a lonely Red heart? Or are you more desperate for a partner than Nando when Rafa plays a 4-5-1? Just call us on 250505.

DUTCH stallion, 29, black mane, FLAH, had trouble scoring in past, OHAS, likes hay, carrots and SL, seeks M/F stable-mate for GRTP and grazing. NSFS as liable to FB.

PHIL, 28, Manc, below average looks, UB, from closely-knit family, new to Merseyside area, WNLTM any SWG.

ANNOYING blonde poseur, 30, looks like cross between AH and LS, recently moved to Blackburn to BNP, likes LIM, aggro, POT every Saturday, seeks female admirers with similar interests to WTGIWO.

KEY:

AFETMTP = anyone famous enough to make the papers
AH = Afghan Hound
AMEX = American Express
AMP = answer my phone
BNP = be nearer parents
BP = butting people
C&A = champagne and aggro
CBF = creosoting back fence
CB = Craig Bellamy
CFM = coat from Matalan
CGSS = could get sacked soon
CLAW = chest like a washboard
CP = chairperson
DA = dark alleyway
DT = drug testers
DW = dog walking
EM = England manager
EFC = Everton Football Club
FAF = fit as ****
FG = former Gladiators
FLAH = face like a horse
FB = fire blanks
FAM = for a month
FAW = for a week
FF = Fat Frank
F&F = football and friendship
GAP = Gary and Phil
GRTP = gallops round the park
GC = gullible chairman
GAJ = gizza job
GITB = getting in the box
GSOH = ginger stalker on heat
HDT = hair dryer treatment
IWP = inflated wage packet
IQ = intelligence quota
LC = Liverpool captain
LIM = looking in mirrors
LLMAY = looks like Magnum and Yozzer
LS = Lily Savage
LTDWM = long term deal worth millions
M/F = mare/filly
M&S = moaning and swearing
NITWIT = not interesting to watch in truth
N/S = non-shaven
NOLNI = name or looks not important
NSFS = not suitable for studding
NUT = Newcastle -Upon-Tyne
OABAAM = Once a Blue always a Manc
OCLWM = own Champions League winner's medal
OHAPC = own house and psychologist's couch
OHAS = own hooves and stables
OKMTB = one knighthood more than Bob
OMAYAFC = own mansion and yacht and football club
OP = occasional pundit
OTAK = own tattoo and kilt
OTS = off the scene
OYCE = one year contract extension
PC = politically correct
PCP = public car park
POT = p*ss*ng off thousands
PS = Posh Spice
RD = romantic dinner
RF = rich footballers
RTTM = respond to text message
SAG = secret agent Johnno
S&M = sausage and mash
SKY = inventors of football
SL = sugar lumps
STR = short term relationship
SSS = sleazy Spanish Senoritas
SWG = Scousers with grudges
TCS = top class striker
TOS = tired old Shearer
TTU = to turn up
TWIT = typical weekend in town
UB = uglier brother
WD = world domination
WNLTM = would not like to meet
WLTB = would like to buy
WLTM = would like to meet
WLTS = would like to s**g
WLTT = would like to text
WTGIWO = worship the ground I walk on
YK = You know

CRRRRRRREEEEEE

MOST Chelski fans, we know, were right behind Liverpool in the Champions League final (no sniggering at the back). But sadly there was a few who didn't take their semi-final defeat in the right spirit. Here's some excerpts from an unofficial Chelski website, written as our fifth European Cup was being won . . .

h3rby
Liverpool are 1-0 down already ...not Crespo though

hernancrespo
Crespo almost scored!

dannyblue
Not bothered about Crespo, just want Milan to win so don't have to face "Champions League you're havin' a larf" from the scousers next season. Come on Milan!!!

Paul M
Stop laughing you lot, he says, wiping tears from his eyes. LOL,LOL,LOL.

Scott Miller
Kewell looks set to come off with a thigh injury. What a waste of money he was.

davidlf
Kewell - the new Darren Anderton???
HA HA HA

h3rby
Crespo!!!!!!!!!!..................2-0

hernancrespo
I've scored!!!!!!!!!!!!!!!!!!!!!!!!!!!!!!!

Paul M
CRRRRRRRREEEEEEEEEEEESSSSSSS
SSSSPPPPPPPPO0000000000000
2-0

johnnysunshine
Goal to Crespo! Come on Chelsea!

Alex K
2-0 2-0. IT'S CRESPO

davidlf
Paying half his wages for a season was well worth that one moment! Well done Crespo - the boy done good! BYE BYE Mickey Mousers - losers in 2 finals, 5th in the league, 37 points behind the CHAMPIONS, they must be sooo proud!

h3rby
omg crespo again!!!!!>..........get in

3-0

dannyblue
hernan crespo hernan crespo oooh oohh hernan crespo hernan crespo. yyyyyyyeeeeeeeeeeessssssssssss!!!!!!!

hernancrespo
Crespo 3-0!

Alex K
I loved that! 'Chelsea's revenge'

Paul M
LOL LOL LOL LOL LOL LOL LOL LOL
Am I going to enjoy work tomorrow.

h3rby
wooooohooo a 4-0 pummelling would be nice. Crespo hat-trick muhahahahaha

Scott M
Sorry lads, I've got a meeting in a couple of minutes and I won't be able to approve any of the second half posts. This isn't the normal match day thread where the posts don't require approval. Hopefully another moderator will be around for the second half. 3-0 at half-time. Silly Silly Scousers! They can add that to their wonderful history!

Jackass1987
Kaka! Kaka! Kaka!

Kaka was amazing! He's superb! Bid for him! 100m!!! Anyway Crespo . . . 2 for Chelsea!

Khobar
Thanks Liverpool - FOR EMBARRASSING THE PREMIER LEAGUE!!

LMAO :-) A few million on Crespo's transfer fee methinks.

h3rby
my bin dipper pal is sayin omg we're playin like Chelsea ahahahahahaha. What a d**k

Jackass1987
Anyway, Rafa got it all wrong! His

line-ups are crappy. Harry Kewell shouldn't be there...instead he should play Cisse. 'Cos he thought he can do a Chelsea against the mighty Milan....sorry mate! I think 2nd half Milan will play it cool...and 'Pool will ...wait. Should attack like crazy

PaulT
So far just what I'd hoped for - resounding proof that (from England's point of view) the wrong team are in the final.

Gary S
Crespo's second goal was stunning, what a pass and finish.

Jackass1987
I keep imagine how is it going to be if Chelsea are playing...Terry taking on Cresp...Carval on Sheva and so on... Anyway Pool's defense is SHAKY tonight. Carragher is nowhere

h3rby
I miss him, bring him back :((

vincent
HaHaHahahHahahahahaHahahahaHAH
AHAHAHAHAHAHAHAHAHAHAHHAHA
and then ROFL

Richard
Poetic justice. Pool were never good enough for the big stage. That's what happens when you get into the realms of fantasy. They were lucky to go through against us.

Alex K
Maybe the fools who so desperately wanted to see the CL come back to England, but cheered on Liverpool against us, will wish so much that it was Chelsea out there now.

h3rby
Ahahahahah. Gerrard almost in tears!!! Priceless!!

h3rby
Crespo hat-trick tellin' ya .... then comes back 2 Bridge in summer as a Blues hero hahaha

h3rby
Gerrard with a header 3-1

SSSSSSSPPPPPPO!

dannyblue
And there goes 5 million on a transfer fee or swap deal.

h3rby
omg Smicer 3-2

Gary S
Can't believe Liverpool got two back.

hernancrespo
Hang on............. 3-2!

Gary S
Liverpool have got a penalty now, what is going on?

h3rby
omg penalty, 3-3 Alonso

Gary S
Missed and then scored the follow up. Liverpool have been outclassed yet somehow are level.

Alex K
I don't believe this....

hernancrespo
Shocking! 3-3!!!!!!!

h3rby
Manic game!! Great final, unlike the bloody FA Cup

dannyblue
Crespo hat-trick anyone??

Paul M
If Liverpool win, I'm going to avoid every newspaper and tv for the next 3 months.

h3rby
omg Liverpool saved, pushed it out and hit off the line

Gary S
Liverpool clear off the line again.

Alex K
You just know Liverpool will win now... If they win it like this... we'll never hear the end of it...

hernancrespo
Come on Milan! Crespo hat-trick will come!

Gary S
There goes Hernan's chance of a hat-trick.

h3rby
No hat-trick, Crespo off :(((booooooo

hernancrespo
And he has been far better than Sheva! Come on Milan!!!

h3rby
Is it gonna go pens if stays this at et or willl it be golden goal??

Paul M
Anyone for penalties? Shame Crespo is not on. They might need him to take one.

blueerato
Hey you Blues, can't you have a little faith and keep the posts coming? It's not like Milan have lost now have they?????? They are gonna score a goal in extra time. Bad thing Crespo is off

Khobar
C'mon Milan for God's sake.

Alex K
I don't know ... Milan have really been shaken by those 3 goals.
I don't care if it goes to pens or not, as long as Milan win.

voodoo
Can't believe no one is commenting on Gerrard's dive for the penalty! Rooney would have been proud of that one.

blue bliz
Is it just me or did Gerrard completely flop to get that penalty? I could have sworn that he was doing a Deco impersonation.

frad
Milan to win on penalties and Stevie OG to miss the decisive one. Would be nice to see that happen....

hernancrespo
Milan are beginning to do my head in. Come on Milan!!!!!!!!!!!!!!!!

Paul M
voodoo and blue bliz, good shout. Thought the same thing. As do alot of people on this site.

dannyblue
PLEASE MILAN so that I don't have to put up with whining scousers singing for the next decade, they've just got over the Eighties. Please!

h3rby
omg off the line again!!!

Paul M
Double save by Dudy. Can see Liverpool winning this on pens.

Gary S
Not by a Gerrard free-kick, please.

h3rby
oh well pens it is

h3rby
omg milan 1 miss 1 saved

h3rby
2-0 on pens to the Pool

hernancrespo
Gosh! Saved!

h3rby
ohhhhhhhhhhhh saved for Milan 2-1

h3rby
2-2 now .... 3-2 Pool

BluSun
This is it.
We will never hear the end of how they won against Milan.I'm hoping for a miracle.

h3rby
omg Shevchenko had his saved.

frad
NO!

Gary S
Liverpool European Champions, what's that all about?

hernancrespo
Goodnite guys! I'm berserk!!!

h3rby
They win it 2 keep, fair play they pld excellent 2nd half well deserved gg:)

Khobar
Appalling - how far off the line was Dudek - how many dodgy decisions? Gutted.

dannyblue
GUTTED. GOD Anfield will be fun

Paul M
Oh well, no newspapers or tv for 3 months then.
DON'T BLOODY WELL BELIEVE IT. NIGHTMARE COME TRUE.
NOOOOOOOOOOOOOOOOOOOOOOOOOOOOOO OOOOOOOOOOOOOOOOO.

subimp555
I feel sick!!!!!!!

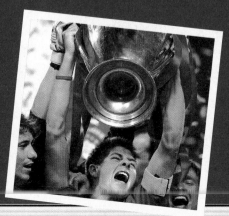

Lucky Liverpool

THE year is 2007 and little bluenose Duncan is talking to his bluenose Dad.

SON: "Dad, my mates in school told me that Liverpool won the European Cup for the fifth time in 2005 – are they right dad?"

DAD: "Yes son, it's true, but they were dead lucky son, all the way through the tournament."

SON: "Why Dad?"

DAD: "Well, in the group stages . . ."

SON: "What Dad, did they have a team from Azerbaijan, Israel, and Ireland in their group?"

DAD: "Well no, they had Monaco, Deportivo La Coruna, and Olympiakos."

SON: "Well they still sound like three easy teams to me Dad . . ."

DAD: "Actually, Monaco reached the final the year before, Olympiakos had won their league seven times out of the previous eight seasons and Deportivo finished above the Galacticos of Real Madrid in their league."

SON: "Jeez Dad, that sounds like quite a difficult group then."

DAD: "Yeh, I suppose you're right, son, but they were still lucky – it took a jammy shot by Gerrard against Olympiakos to get them through."

SON: "Is that the goal where your hero Andy Gray shouts: 'You beauty, you beauty, what a hit son, what a hit!'"

DAD: "Yes son it is."

SON: "Oh, okay. Well, what happened in the last 16 dad, who did they draw?"

DAD: "Bayer Leverkusen."

SON: "Bayer who?"

DAD: "Exactly son, but they had beaten Real Madrid 3-0 at home, and won their group that included Dinamo Kiev and Roma too."

SON: "Bloody hell Dad, they sound good!"

DAD: "Yes, I suppose you're right son"

SON: "So did they win on away goals or something?"

DAD: "Errrrr, no, they won both legs 3-1."

SON: "Oh well, who did they get next then Dad?"

DAD: "Juventus."

SON: "How the hell did they get past them Dad?"

DAD: "Well, they did – they won 2-1 at home, and cruised to a 0-0 away draw without Juve having hardly a chance."

SON: "Were Juve crap at that time – had all their decent players gone or something?"

DAD: "Well, actually, they still had players like Del Piero, Nedved, Ibrahimovic, Thuram, and Buffon in the side. And they won Serie A a few weeks later."

SON: "Wow, they beat the Italian champions elect - which dead easy team did they get in the semi then?"

DAD: "Chelsea."

SON: "Chelsea – oh for God's sake – what an easy draw – they've won nothing. Everton have won more than them."

DAD: "Well that season they won the Premiership and League Cup but the Red ***** didn't let them score in 180 minutes of football."

SON: "I don't believe it – so Liverpool beat the English champions elect too?"

DAD: "Yes son, they bloody well did."

SON: "So, after all that, I suppose all the good teams had been knocked out?"

DAD: "Not quite son, AC Milan awaited them in the final."

SON: "No way – aren't they the second most successful team in the competition?"

DAD: "Yes son they are."

SON: "So were Liverpool lucky because Milan had all their good players out with injuries?"

DAD: "No – they had Shevchenko, Crespo, Maldini, Nesta, Cafu, Kaka, Stam, Dida, Gattuso, Pirlo, and Seedorf."

SON: "You're 'avin a laff!"

DAD: "It gets worse son! Milan were cruising 3-0 up at half-time . . ."

SON: "What happened? Did they have three men sent off in the second half – how did Liverpool get back into the game?"

DAD: "No, Milan had no men sent off, the Red ***** scored 3 goals in 6 minutes!"

SON: "Against the best defence in Europe?"

DAD: "Yes! Against the best defence in Europe!"

SON: "So what happened next. Extra time?"

DAD: "Yes son, and Dudek made the luckiest save ever to stop a Shevchenko shot from a yard."

SON: "Why was it lucky dad – did it hit him on the bum, nose, shoulder or something"

DAD: "No son, his hand . . ."

SON: "Well, aren't goalies meant to save shots with their hands?"

DAD: "Yeah but that's besides the point!"

SON: "Then what . . ."

DAD: "Penalties!"

SON: "English teams are crap at penalties."

DAD: "Not this time they weren't – they only missed one. And that's how Liverpool became the luckiest team to win the European Cup."

SON: "But I bet when they brought the cup home there was hardly anyone to watch as all Liverpool fans live anywhere but Liverpool you say. How many was there, 5,000 or so?"

DAD: "1 million people lined the streets."

SON: "So, let's get this straight Dad . . . Liverpool had three good teams in their group, they then knocked out a team who had beaten Real Madrid 3-0, they then knocked out the future Serie A champions, then knocked out the future Premiership champions, before coming back from 3-0 down to beat the second most successful club in Europe. And then the whole population of Liverpool came out to welcome them home!"

DAD: "That about sums it up son"

SON: "Dad?"

DAD: "Yes son?"

SON: "Can I have a Liverpool shirt for my birthday next week, and can you stop calling me Duncan – I'm Stevie from now on."

Anonymous (Taken from the internet, post-Istanbul, 2005)

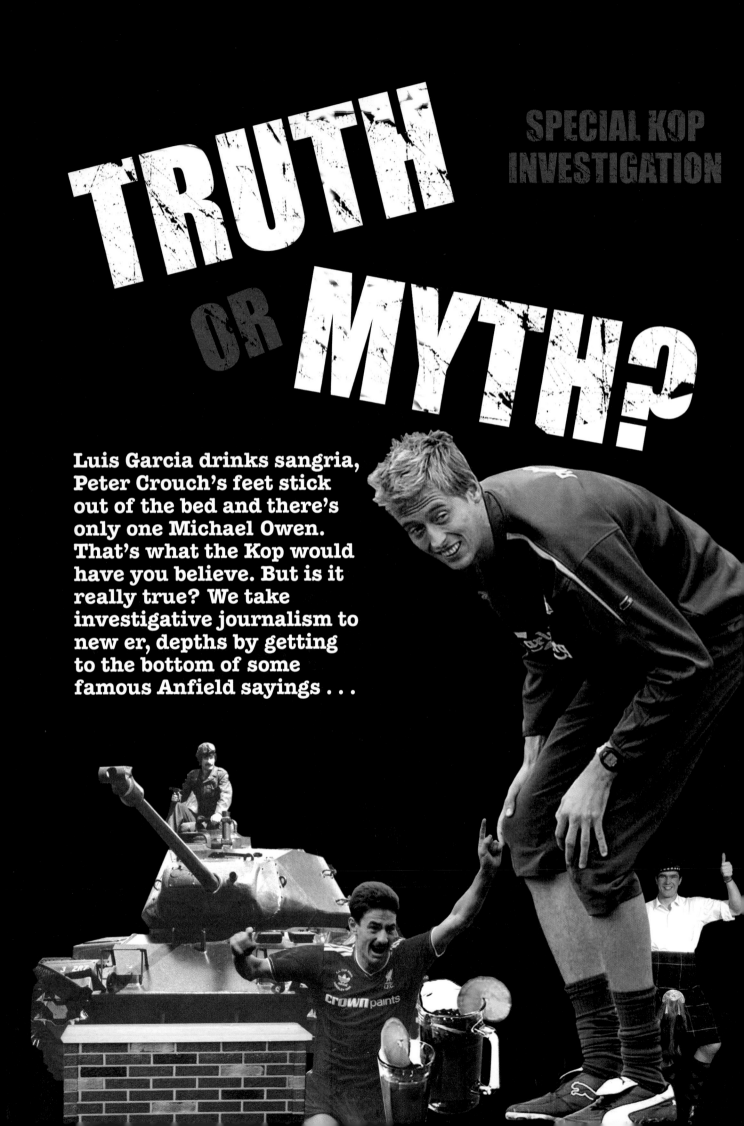

TRUTH OR MYTH?

Luis Garcia drinks sangria, Peter Crouch's feet stick out of the bed and there's only one Michael Owen. That's what the Kop would have you believe. But is it really true? We take investigative journalism to new er, depths by getting to the bottom of some famous Anfield sayings . . .

' THERE'S ONLY ONE MICHAEL OWEN

(Famous Kop chant celebrating the unique Welsh superstar)

Loneliness of the Long-dis

Evening Standard (London), January
by Michael Owen

Kenneth Branagh's four-hour epic f
present life

It is mid morning and Ken Branagh ha
in,' he says almost guiltily, pulling hard

He looks like an everyday Joe in a nor
last year replaced by his own reddish,

MAIN PAGE
Michael Owen

Actor :

Denotes a New York Times Critic's Pic

1988	Little Nikita	A C B
1945	Mr. Muggs Rides Again	A
1945	Over 21	A

Investigation findings: As our pictures clearly show, the name 'Michael Owen' is far from unique. Indeed, the Welsh rugby union team boasts a sportsman of the same name and a Google internet search reveals others sharing the same title including a stunt actor and respected late newspaper arts editor.

DISPROVED

 # LUIS GARCIA, HE DRINKS SANGRIA

('He came from Barca to bring us joy . . .' Kop song '05)

 +  =

Investigation findings: This song was given hearty renditions in the bars of Istanbul but it appears the drink may have been talking here. A reliable source informs us that Luis is, in fact, the ultimate professional – and never touches a drop.

DISPROVED

' IAN, IAN RUSH: HE GETS THE
, BALL AND SCORES A GOAL

(Famous terrace song in celebration of prolific Welsh hitman)

Investigation findings: He moved so fast it always seems like there was two of him - hence the 'Ian, Ian Rush' bit of the song. Our picture, above left, proves this to be true. In our random research, we also asked a Mr B. Mimms and Mr N. Southall about the claim that Ian Rush always scored when he had the ball   and they confirmed this to be the case.

PROVED

' HE'S CZECH, HE'S GREAT, ' HE'S PADDY BERGER'S MATE'

(Famous Kop chant in honour of ex-Red Vladimir Smicer)

missing

Best mate me arse

Investigation findings: Vladi was definitely Czech and after Istanbul, many would not deny the claim that he was great. But it is unconfirmed if Paddy Berger is still his mate after he failed to return an alice band that he borrowed earlier this year - forcing his Czech mate into wearing a hat to keep his flowing locks under control whilst training.

' TOMMY SMITH WOULD RUN THROUGH ' A BRICK WALL FOR LIVERPOOL

(Famous Kop saying for legendary Anfield hard man Tommy Smith)

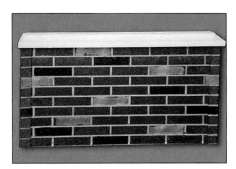

Investigation findings: There weren't many things that stood in the way of Anfield Iron Tommy Smith during his playing days. But when he was faced with the challenge of running head on through a brick wall, he used his head - and lined up a tank to do the job instead.

' IN ISTANBUL, WE WON IT FIVE TIMES '

(New Kop song to celebrate the arrival of our fifth European Cup in Turkey)

1977

1978

1981

1984

2005

Investigation findings: Kopites were witnessed coming out of the Ataturk stadium on May 25, 2005 saying: 'Did that really happen?' and mumbling 'unbelievable . . . unbelievable'. Well, it did happen (unless you left at half-time). And for those of you watching in Manchester, here are the other years we won it in: 1977, 1978, 1981, 1984.

'HE'S BIG, HE'S RED, HIS FEET STICK OUT THE BED, PETER CROUCH'

(New Kop song for Rafa's and Liverpool's biggest ever signing)

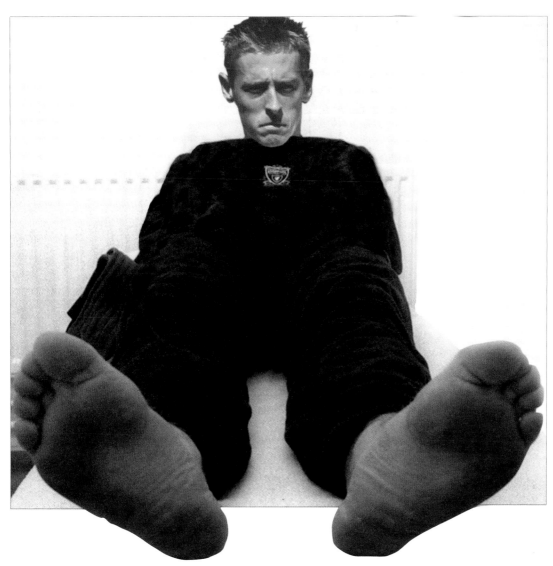

Investigation findings: The Kop weren't slow in coming up with a big hit for our new boy. But are they off the mark in suggesting he is too tall for the average bed? At 6ft 7ins, Peter measures nearly half an inch more than the normal 75-80 inch mattress, so this would indeed appear to be the case. Spot on lads!

'RON YEATS IS ABOUT 7 FOOT TALL'

(Famous Bill Shankly quote about former Liverpool captain)

Crouchy

Big Ron
Stevie G
Flo

Investigation findings: Still on the Peter Crouch theme, here's one tall story too many told by Shanks. The great man once claimed Ron Yeats was about 7 foot tall but as our graphic shows, the Scot comes nowhere near the 6ft 7ins Peter Crouch (even when he's Crouching). And all this despite the Anfield defender from the '60s donning his country's traditional dress.

KOP EFC TV guide

MON

little angels

9am: Little Angells: Can Brett's children miss as many chances as he could?

10am: FILM: Honey, I Shrunk the Kids: Pat Nevin's Dad has some explaining to do.

12pm: Little Britain: Every village has got one. We search for an Evertonian in Llandewi Breffi.

LLANDDEWI-BREFI

TUE

7am: The Clangers: With Sandy Brown

8.30am: Looney Tunes: The Gwladys Street regulars reveal their latest chant for Duncan Ferguson.

DOCUMENTARY

10am: Without a Trace: Whatever happened to Wayne Clarke? And Mike Milligan? And Carl Tiler?

12.30pm: Cash in the Attic: Richard Wright reveals what he was really looking for when he dislocated his shoulder in his parents' attic

WED

8.30am: Pigeon Street: An insight into where Duncan Ferguson lives.

10am: Walking with Dinosaurs: Tony Hibbert reveals what it's like to play in the same team as David Weir and Nigel Martyn.

2.30pm: Everybody Loves Raymond: A profile of Ray Atteveld's glorious Everton career

2.30pm: Nip/Tuck: James Beattie tries a new method of getting into shape.

THUR

9.30am: Animal Hospital: Joe Royle's dogs of war visit the School of Science – but the operation isn't a success

10.30am: Bargain Hunt: David Moyes searches for the next Eddie Bosnar.

11am: The Salon: The team attempt to cut John Bailey's hair (subsequent programmes may run late)

FRI

6pm: The Simonsens: At home with the goalkeeper Walter Smith paid £3.3 million for (programme may feature Evertonians saying 'd'oh!')

8pm: The Apprentice: Everton's Academy stars battle it out for a place in the first team and a subsequent multi-million pound transfer to a bigger club.

9.30pm: Gimme Gimme Gimm Tim Cahill's agent sits down for contract talks with Bill Kenwright.

SAT

10am: Howard's Way: Howard tells the story of how he would have won the European Cup if it wasn't for Liverpool fans. (repeat)

10.15am: Time Team Special: The archaeologists visit Goodison Park and begin searching for any last traces of silver.

7pm: Blind Date: David Moyes meets the latest batch of Thai trialists that have been sent to Bellefield

SUN

11am: Songs of Praise: The congregation in St Luke's Church on the corner of Goodison Park outsing the Gwladys Street faithful (repeat)

CLASSIC

1pm: FILM: Carry on Abroad: How things worked out for Gary Lineker when he quit Goodison for the Nou Camp.

5pm: Escape to the Country: Wayne Rooney reveals why he decided to relocate to Alderley Edge (programme will contain b language)

Don't know what to watch on telly tonight? Why not tune in to Toffee TV and see how the other half live. From Bargain Hunt and the search for the next Eddy Bosnar to (You) Beauty and the Beast with Andy Gray and Richard Keys, there's something for everyone!

1pm: Wimbledon '88: A look where David Moyes got his tactical inspiration from.

4pm: University Challenge: Part 3,951. We continue the search for an Evertonian with a degree.

6pm: Rising Damp: An in-depth look at the Bullens Road stand.

9pm: Men Behaving Badly: With Duncan Ferguson. And James Beattie. And Billy Kenny. And Mark Ward.

10.30pm: FILM. The Great Spain Robbery. Starring Telly Savalas as Pierluigi Collina and Sally Gunnell as Diego Forlan.

PICK OF THE DAY

5.35pm: Neighbours: A look at what your average Evertonian dislikes about Liverpool FC (subsequent programmes may run very, very late)

7pm: You Are What You Eat: This week - eating too much rubbish. With James Beattie.

9pm: The Royle Family: Head of the family, Big Joe, looks for a new home with high ceilings in Ipswich.

9pm: New Tricks: Flying but balding winger Ian Wilson shows off his full-range of full-back beating tricks.

9.01pm: Crimewatch UK. Featuring Mark Ward and Mickey Thomas.

11pm: FILM: The Secret Agent. 'Red Johnno' takes charge at Goodison Park.

7.01pm: FILM: The Great Escape (1994): Starring Hans Segers.

KICK OF THE DAY

9pm: Beavis and Butthead: With James Beattie and William Gallas.

9.30pm: Tonight with Neil McDonald: The former Everton defender presents a hard-hitting investigation into how he made over 100 appearances for the Blues.

10pm: Two Pints of Lager and a Packet of Crisps: Paul Gascoigne talks about pre-match meals (subtitles available).

8pm: Cold Feet: Andy Gray re-lives the time when he said he'd take the Everton manager's job in '97 and make Dwight Yorke his first signing but got offered more money by Sky and stayed there.

12am: FILM: Se7en: Thriller. Filmed on location at Highbury in May 2005, not starring Richard Wright or his back four.

9.30pm: The Fast Show. Not featuring Alan Stubbs or David Unsworth.

MISS OF THE DAY

11pm: FILM: Catch 22: A look back at all the saves Paul Gerrard made in his Everton career.

12am: Top Gear: The Police reveal what they found when they raided Mark Ward's house.

6pm: FILM: (You) Beauty and the Beast: With Andy Gray and Richard Keys.

8pm: CSI: Crime Scene Investigation. The bizzies finally get round to examining the Wimbledon team bus that spontaneously combusted before that relegation decider in 1994.

9pm: I'm a Celebrity Get Me Out of Here: David Ginola recalls his time at Goodison Park.

It's a re-sit of the Russian exam at school but once again Steven Gerrard refuses to put pen to paper

Young pals Mikey Robinson (aged 11) and Alan Kennedy (aged 12) visit the club museum as fans. Little did they know that one day they would play for the Reds

So that's where Mighty Mouse got his great balance from! Kevin Keegan earns some extra pocket money on the streets of Doncaster by hanging spoons on his nose

★ *Before they were* FAMOUS

We've unearthed some embarrassing pictures of young Anfield wannabees before they became Kop idols...

Getting a haircut was always a possibility for 16-year-old Rafa Benitez. But he did have options with the girls. He was under pressure from his mates to go for a real striking one, but a right laugh and getting the closed-down youth centre back were his priorities

A taste of things to come. El Tosh and senor Hall head for Flamenco classes on the University campus

Trainee butcher Peter Thompson found it easier and more enjoyable carving up defences than a pig's arse

Bubble King Kenny goes head to head with rival Bob Latchford at the annual Youth Club World Cup

All your Anfield queries answered. No question too big or small!

You Ask, We Answer

I HAVE enjoyed the many different tributes that have been paid to European champions Liverpool over the course of 2005 but I fear the confectionery powers-that-be have missed a trick.

Wouldn't it be both tasty and appropriate if Kit-Kat makers added an extra chocolate finger to their already popular bar in celebration of the Reds' fifth continental crown.

I believe this would be a fitting and mouth-watering addition to newsagents' sweet shelves in this historic year and could also be sold in the club's snack bar alongside Turkish Delight in honour of our Istanbul heroes.

C. Hoc-O'holic,
Diehard Red

A: I'd love to give you the one finger you deserve for those ideas.

I BUMPED into a Jari Litmanen lookalike in our local newsagents. He was buying 20 Benson & Hedges and a packet of extra strong mints. Do I win a prize?

Brian Straw-Clutcher,
Hants

A: Didn't you write in last year? The answer's still no.

OFFICE workers who start at nine should now finish at five in honour of our 2005 triumph. This may result in additional traffic congestion but I believe it would be worth it as a white-collared celebration of our amazing fifth continental crown.

F. Witt, Orrell Park

A: Surely this would result in a mass exodus which is the last thing employers or traffic chiefs would want.

IT is worth bearing in mind that not all Kopites are better off after this summer's Champions League success.

I, for one, have had to resort to cycling to work as I can't find a single petrol station in the city that sells five-star.

S. Adlad, Merseyside

A: Sad but true.

WOULDN'T it be great if Rock'n'Roll legend Noddy Holder was a Red? The Slade front man could be pictured with our European Cup under the headline: 'Noddy and Ol' Big Ears'.

Via e-mail

A: Sadly I believe he's a Brummie, so he's more likely to be a Manc. Maybe we could get Doddy instead?

I MANAGED to sneak on the Liverpool team photo when they won the European Cup. Do I win anything for my efforts?

S. Diao, Senegal

A: Yes, a Champions League winner's medal.

I HAVE recently become aware that Liverpool's Spanish full-back 'Josemi' is in fact called Jose Miguel Gonzalez Rey but shortened it by simply taking the first six letters of his full name.

This was, in my opinion, a clever idea for name-on-shirt fitting purposes and I now plan to do the same with my name.

Wan Kerry Choi Park,
South Korea

A: Please explain this to the staff at the club shop when ordering your shirt or you risk causing offence.

FANS who wear jester's hats to games? They're all tw*ts in my book.

R. Eelfan, Toxteth

A: It's regrettable that you don't appreciate the light-heartedness behind this Shakesperean-inspired matchday headwear. (But you're dead right).

I REGRET to have to say it but I believe Liverpool are sadly misguided when it comes to building a new stadium in Stanley Park.

The toilet facilities are simply not up to coping with the number of fans and I believe dog-fouling would cause players to lose their footing at vital moments.

Who's also to say that a vagrant under the influence of a morning on the Diamond White might not prove a hazard when Fernando Morientes is lumbering into the penalty area?

Instead, why not consider the option of an adjacent piece of green space. Goodison Park is relatively unused and will provide an ample footballing area which comes ready equipped with seating.

I realise the colour scheme may not be suitable but the title of 'The People's Club' is something the great Shanks could have thought of himself.

Penny Wise, Aigburth

A: Wise words, Penny. Why don't we share the ground with another team too? I think you should start a debate in the Echo.

ARE the fans who sing 'we all dream of a team of Carraghers' completely stupid?

Until his strike in Lithuania Jamie had not scored a single goal since 1999 which means that if we had a team full of Carraghers we would have gone almost 40,000 minutes without scoring a goal.

This would have constituted a world record and I believe winning a fifth European Cup under such circumstances would have proved to be very difficult.

Anne Orak, Macclesfield

A: We wouldn't let any goals in though and could make a fortune from backing 0-0 with the bookies.

MY Mum reckons that my favourite band, the Beatles, once played at Anfield. Is this true?

N. Gallagher,
Burnage, Manchester

A: Yes. But they were beaten 164-0 as they only fielded a four-man team.

I AM livid after a gang of Scousers camped on my land and left several of my prize bulls scarred for life. They left some mystery markings on each of the poor beasts. Who do these people think they are?

Getorf Myland,
Farmer for 128 years, Wales

A: European champions?

I HAVE always agreed that no one man is bigger than the club but I was sat on the back row of the Upper Centenary Stand the other week and realised that I still had to look up to see Peter Crouch's head. Do you think we should now build an extra tier on the new stadium to preserve this old Liverpool adage?

Ivor Gudpoint,
Iceland

A: No.

You can't beat a bit of Istan-bully . . .

✐ THEY say that if the wind turns while you are pulling a funny face it will stick. I remember Mark Lawrenson eating a lolly ice with some of the other Liverpool players and it was so cold on his teeth it made him wince and say "ooooh" in a high-pitched voice. At that very moment there was a reversal in the direction of a stiff breeze and to his horror Lawro's tone and expression became a permanent fixture. I've heard on the grapevine that you have a picture of the incident.

I. C. Lolly
Blackpool

A: You're quite right, as the picture above clearly shows.

✐ I WOKE up one morning in 1978 to find two men in my garden chopping down my beloved 73-year-old oak trees. One of them was a Scouser with a 'tache but they scarpered before I could apprehend them. I just wondered if you had any pictures of the culprits?

L. Umberjaque
Nottingham Forest

A: Are these the tree fellers, sorry two fellas you're after (above)?

✐ I AM trying to trace my family tree and believe that a current member of my family could be in the Liverpool area. After much searching I tracked him down to Germany but was told that I was a few years late and he was now in Liverpool. If you know of Alou's whereabouts please can you pass my address on to him? Thanks.

Pierre Diarra,
France

A: Alou Diarra? Doesn't ring a bell here. Sorry we can't help

✐ AS the man who personally discovered that the Nazis were trying to make blond-haired blue-eyed clones during the war I was horrified to stumble across something similar going on behind the scenes at Anfield early in 1974. Dr Von Yeats was trying to clone the perfect defender is his secret lab in Scotland. The prototype was called 'The Hansen'. I still have the secret documents I managed to acquire at the time, somewhere safe, in a safe. As far as I am aware their evil experiment never worked thanks to my intervention. Thought you might like to show your readers my top secret picture of the 'The Hansen'

Arsene Vengler
London

A: Gosh, imagine if they had pulled it off!

✐ MY husband claims that Harry Kewell played in both the Carling Cup and Champions League finals in 2005. I say he didn't. Please could you tell us who is right.

Sheree Kewell,
Cheshire

A: The statistics show that he was selected for both games but we can't remember him playing in either so you're right.

*Brought to you in association with the bloke who irons that giant Champions League flag and then goes mad when a bunch of kids shake it in the centre circle...

* WHEN in Manchester playing golf and you're about to hit a local resident with a wayward drive, now shout 'Five!' instead of 'Fore' to make them even more angry
.

Gerrinda Hole, India

* WHEN in Manchester playing golf don't ask a local the way to the 18th as they've only ever got as far as the 15th and wouldn't know where to go after that.

Ho Lin Wan, Thailand

* GET Sky commentator Andy Gray to judge the Miss Liverpool contest and listen to him shout 'You Beauty' as each of the contestants are paraded.

A. Gray, Closet Kopite

* GET a free pint in Aldo's Place by going in dressed as Quasimodo and telling him you used to play up front together for Liverpool in the 1980s.

H. Unchback, Notre Dame

* IF you can't get to a game then re-create the pre-match Anfield atmosphere by recording Phil Easton's Magic 1548 breakfast show and playing his pointless chit-chat back for 30 minutes before putting You'll Never Walk Alone on at five to three.

D.J. George, Sefton

* FIND out how long it takes before the human body transforms into a skeleton by trying to purchase a ticket on L.F.C's credit card hotline.

Thisisa B.T. Announcement

* GET yer hats, caps, scarves flags, badges wristbands or yer souvenir Champions League t-shirts by approaching a man shouting such things near the exit to Stanley Park.

H.C.S Anyerbage

* GET into Anfield for free by turning up two hours before kick-off in a flourescent orange or yellow coat and telling people to 'sit down' and 'keep the stairway clear'.

Stu Ward, Garston

* MAKE yourself a lot of money by selling the shares in your beloved football club to a wealthy American businessman and then going supporting Chelski because they're now more successful.

Johnny Come Lately, Kent

* SEE the European Cup every day of your life by wearing the same clothes you had on in Istanbul and donating yourself to the Anfield museum where you will be kept in a large glass case and viewed by a stream of tourists.

Mannie Quinn, Liverpool 5

* CASH in with an ivory dealer by stealing Ronaldo and Ronaldinho's front teeth and claim they came from elephants you captured at Knowsley Safari Park.

A Hunter, Huyton

* SET up a football team in Ireland and be guaranteed capacity crowds every week by naming it The Craic FC. The fans would flock to watch the games because everybody in Ireland loves the Craic.

Toby Shaw, Too Bay Shore

* INSTEAD of just singing 'Ring Of Fire', why not experience one for yourself. Simply eat a bag of green chillies at haf time rather than your usual Wagon Wheel. (*Please note: Bring a radio to the match to keep up to date on the second half action).

J. Nash, Cashville

* REALLY annoy the Department of Employment by applying for a work permit when you know you're eligible to play in England - thus forcing them into doing extra paperwork to ensure your rightful claim is denied.

M. Gonzalez, Chile

* CREATE your historic Arsenal shirt and earn a fortune by submerging a white T-shirt in a sinkful of Ribena and then selling it to gullible Gunners.

D. Dein, N. London

KOP CARTOON

MILAN'S got his bag packed and Anthony Le Tallec's heading out on loan as Flo, Crouchy, Mellor, Cisse and Morientes start the season at Melwood. Room for one more striker before the transfer window closes? Er . . . no.

CRIMEFILE 05

The accused is pictured leaving the scene of the crime with the most valuable silverware in Europe. He had a plane waiting for him at Istanbul airport and was later spotted by police on the top deck of a bus in Merseyside. He was escorted to St George's Hall for questioning ——

STATEMENT: 'I won it in a competition mate!'

WITNESSES: 80,000 ~~Scousers~~

PREVIOUS CONVICTIONS: Part of the LFC family still wanted by Interpol (now known as AC-pol) for similar offences in Rome 1977, London 1978, Paris 1981, Rome 1984

Name: Steven GerrArd

DOB: 30 /05 /1980   Received: _-_/_-_/_-_   Age: 25

County: Nr.AttURk Std. Istanbul   Date of offense: 25 /05 /2005

Age at time of offense: 24

Weight: Of team on shoulders   Eyes: BlooDshot   Hair: Full of chaMpaGne   Height: He's big and hArd

Native County: EnGland   State: LIVerPooL

Prior Occupation: Olympiakos Hijacker   Education level: WoRld CLAss

CASE CLOSED

champions of europe pub quiz

1. Which three Liverpool players featured in all 15 of the Champions League fixtures?

2. Milan Baros and Steve Finnan played in 14 of the 15 games. Name the matches they missed.

3. Which two Liverpool players scored Champions League goals against teams from their home nations?

4. Name the AK Grazer player who got booked twice in the same game at Anfield but wasn't sent off.

5. Who was the only player to be sent off in a Champions League game involving Liverpool in 2004/05?

6. Which Liverpool player said after the final in Istanbul: "When I got back to the hotel I lit a huge cigar. It was huge. I kept puffing it and lighting it up and it never went out. I did not get any sleep at all."

7. Two Brazilians and two Argentinians scored against Liverpool during their Champions League campaign. Name them.

8. What nationality was the linesman who judged Luis Garcia's winner against Chelski to have croseed the line.

9. Before the shoot-out in Istanbul, Liverpool were awarded just one penalty, which they missed, in the whole of their Champions League campaign. Who took it?

10. Excluding the qualifier against AK Grazer, what was unusual about the three Champions League goals Liverpool conceded at Anfield?

Answers: Opposite

mad taxi for . . .

. . . early leavers in Istanbul! One of Istanbul's crazy cabs was where you'll have been sat if you left the Ataturk Stadium at half-time and missed the most famous six minutes of football in Liverpool Football Club and European football's entire history. Still, at least the beer was cheap eh?

liver-pool table

England's European Cup winners:

Liverpool 5, Notts Forest 2, Man Ure 2, Aston Villa 1, Chelski 0, Arsenal 0, Everton 0, Wigan Athletic 0, Southport 0, Prescot Cables 0, Royal Engineers 0, Newcastle 0, Chelski 0, Arsenal 0 (whaddya mean we've already mentioned them?)

get FIVE in for

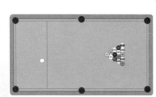

on the oche

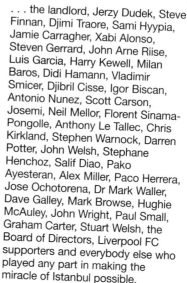

. . . the landlord, Jerzy Dudek, Steve Finnan, Djimi Traore, Sami Hyypia, Jamie Carragher, Xabi Alonso, Steven Gerrard, John Arne Riise, Luis Garcia, Harry Kewell, Milan Baros, Didi Hamann, Vladimir Smicer, Djibril Cisse, Igor Biscan, Antonio Nunez, Scott Carson, Josemi, Neil Mellor, Florent Sinama-Pongolle, Anthony Le Tallec, Chris Kirkland, Stephen Warnock, Darren Potter, John Welsh, Stephane Henchoz, Salif Diao, Pako Ayesteran, Alex Miller, Paco Herrera, Jose Ochotorena, Dr Mark Waller, Dave Galley, Mark Browse, Hughie McAuley, John Wright, Paul Small, Graham Carter, Stuart Welsh, the Board of Directors, Liverpool FC supporters and everybody else who played any part in making the miracle of Istanbul possible.

pub menu

Special:
Turkish
Delight

pub tune

To the tune of
'Yellow Submarine'
by The Beatles

We all dream of a
team of Carraghers,
A team of Carraghers,
A team of Carraghers.
We all dream of a
team of Carraghers,
A team of Carraghers,
A team of Carraghers.

Number one is Carragher,
Number two is Carragher,
Number three is Carragher,
Number four is Carragher.

We all dream of a
team of Carraghers,
A team of Carraghers,
A team of Carraghers.
We all dream of a
team of Carraghers,
A team of Carraghers,
A team of Carraghers.

Number five is Carragher,
Number six is Carragher,
Number seven is Carragher,
Number eight is Carragher.

We all dream of a
team of Carraghers,
A team of Carraghers,
A team of Carraghers.
We all dream of a
team of Carraghers,
A team of Carraghers,
A team of Carraghers.

Number nine is Carragher,
Number 10 is Carragher,
Number 11 is Carragher,
And number 12 is Carragher.

We all dream of a
team of Carraghers,
A team of Carraghers,
A team of Carraghers.
We all dream of a
team of Carraghers,
A team of Carraghers,
A team of Carraghers.

Number 13 is Carragher,
Number 14 is Carragher,
Number 15 is Carragher,
Number 16 is Carragher.

We all dream of a
team of Carraghers,
A team of Carraghers,
A team of Carraghers.
We all dream of a
team of Carraghers,
A team of Carraghers,
A team of Carraghers.

Carra FC's

STAT BAR

		H/A	RES	ATT	SCORER	M.O.M
July						
13	TNS (CL Q1) 1st	H	0-0	55,555	-	Carragher
19	TNS (CL Q1) 2nd	H	0-0	55,555	-	Carragher
26	FBK Kaunas (CL Q2) 1st	A	1-0	55,555	Carra	Carragher
August						
2	FBK Kaunas (CL Q2) 2nd	H	0-0	55,555	-	Carragher
10	CSKA Sofia (CL Q3) 1st	A	0-0	55,555	-	Carragher
13	Middlesbrough	A	0-0	55,555	-	Carragher
20	Sunderland	H	0-0	55,555	-	Carragher
23	CSKA Sofia (CL Q3) 2nd	H	0-0	55,555	-	Carragher
26	CSKA Moscow (SC)	N	0-0	55,555	-	Carragher
September						
10	Tottenham	A	0-0	55,555	-	Carragher
13	Real Betis (CL group 1	A	0-0	55,555	-	Carragher
18	Man USA	H	0-0	55,555	-	Carragher
24	Birmingham	A	0-0	55,555	-	Carragher
28	Chelsea (CL group 2)	H	0-0	55,555	-	Carragher
October						
2	Chelski	H	0-0	55,555	-	Carragher
15	Blackburn	H	0-0	55,555	-	Carragher
19	Anderlecht (CL group 3)	A	0-0	55,555	-	Carragher
22	Fulham	A	0-0	55,555	-	Carragher
25/26	Carling Cup 3rd		0-0	55,555	-	Carragher
29	West Ham	H	0-0	55,555	-	Carragher
November						
1	Anderlecht (CL group 4)	H	0-0	55,555	-	Carragher
5	Aston Villa	A	0-0	55,555	-	Carragher
19	Portsmouth	H	0-0	55,555	-	Carragher
23	Real Betis (CL group 5)	H	0-0	55,555	-	Carragher
26	Man City	A	0-0	55,555	-	Carragher
29/30	Carling Cup 4th		0-0	55,555	-	Carragher
December						
3	Wigan	H	0-0	55,555	-	Carragher
6	Chelsea (CL group 6)	A	0-0	55,555	-	Carragher
10	Middlesbrough	H	0-0	55,555	-	Carragher
15	Sydney/D Sap (WCC SF)	N	0-0	55,555	-	Carragher
17	Sunderland	A	0-0	55,555	-	Carragher
18	WCC final or 3rdp/o	N	0-0	55,555	-	Carragher
20/21	Carling Cup QF		0-0	55,555	-	Carragher
26	Newcastle	H	0-0	55,555	-	Carragher
28	Everton	A	0-0	55,555	-	Carragher
31	West Brom	H	0-0	55,555	-	Carragher
January						
2	Bolton	A	0-0	55,555	-	Carragher
7	FA Cup 3rd		0-0	55,555	-	Carragher
10/11	Carling Cup SF1		0-0	55,555	-	Carragher
14	Tottenham	H	0-0	55,555	-	Carragher
21	Man USA	A	0-0	55,555	-	Carragher
24/25	Carling Cup SF2		0-0	55,555	-	Carragher
28	FA Cup 4th		0-0	55,555	-	Carragher
31	Birmingham	H	0-0	55,555	-	Carragher
February						
4	Chelski	A	0-0	55,555	-	Carragher
11	Wigan	A	0-0	55,555	-	Carragher
18	FA Cup 5th		0-0	55,555	-	Carragher
21/22	CL last 16 1st		0-0	55,555	-	Carragher
25	Man City	H	0-0	55,555	-	Carragher
26	Carling Cup Final (Cardiff)	N	0-0	55,555	-	Carragher
March						
4	Charlton	H	0-0	55,555	-	Carragher
7/8	CL last 16 2nd		0-0	55,555	-	Carragher
11	Arsenal	A	0-0	55,555	-	Carragher
18	Newcastle	A	0-0	55,555	-	Carragher
20-23	FA Cup QF		0-0	55,555	-	Carragher
25	Everton	H	0-0	55,555	-	Carragher
28/29	CL QF 1st		0-0	55,555	-	Carragher
April						
1	West Brom	A	0-0	55,555	-	Carragher
4/5	CL QF 2nd		0-0	55,555	-	Carragher
9	Bolton	H	0-0	55,555	-	Carragher
15	Blackburn	A	0-0	55,555	-	Carragher
17	Fulham	H	0-0	55,555	-	Carragher
18/19	CL SF 1st		0-0	55,555	-	Carragher
22	FA Cup SF		0-0	55,555	-	Carragher
22	West Ham	A	0-0	55,555	-	Carragher
25/26	CL SF 2nd		0-0	55,555	-	Carragher
29	Aston Villa	H	0-0	55,555	-	Carragher
May						
7	Portsmouth	A	0-0	55,555	-	Carragher
13	FA Cup final (Wembley)	N	0-0	55,555	-	Carragher
17	CL Final (Paris)	N	0-0	55,555	-	Carragher
TBC	Arsenal	H	(No need to arrange as we think			
TBC	Charlton	A	we know how the results will finish)			

Number 17 is Carragher,
Number 18 is Carragher,
Number 19 is Carragher
Number 20 is Carragher.

We all dream of a
team of Carraghers,
A team of Carraghers,
A team of Carraghers.
We all dream of a
team of Carraghers,
A team of Carraghers,
A team of Carraghers.

Number 21 is Carragher,
Number 22 is Carragher,
Number 23 is Carragher,
The whole team is Carragher!

We all dream of a
team of Carraghers,
A team of Carraghers,
A team of Carraghers.

We all dream of a
team of Carraghers,
A team of Carraghers,
A TEAM OF
CARRAGHERS!

Repeat for as long and as
loud as your vocal chords
will let you . . .

champions league pub quiz answers